THE WORKSHOP APPROACH TO CLASSROOM INTEREST CENTERS:

A Teacher's Handbook of Learning Games and Activities

- the mechanics and explanation of how to set up learning centers
- scores of illustrations for easier and faster reading and understanding

You'll discover how to make these centers an integral part of the school day. You'll see how all students, slow or fast, will work and learn better through the structure of the interest center or workshop.

Here is the book that can do it for you—bring life into your daily school lessons and show children what they can discover, explore, and develop of their own natural talents.

The authors themselves have developed, tested, and revised the material presented, thus assuring you of its practicality. Now, they invite you to share their exceptional educational findings!

THE WORKSHOP APPROACH TO CLASSROOM INTEREST CENTERS:

A Teacher's Handbook of Learning Games and Activities

Barbara Kilroy Ingram
Nancy Riggs Jones
Marlene LeButt

Illustrated by Barbara Kilroy Ingram

Parker Publishing Company, Inc., West Nyack, N.Y.

© 1975, *by*

PARKER PUBLISHING COMPANY, INC.
West Nyack, N.Y.

Library of Congress Cataloging in Publication Data

Ingram, Barbara Kilroy,
    The workshop approach to classroom interest cen-
ters.

    Includes index.
    1. Educational games. 2. Creative activities
and seat work. I. Jones, Nancy Riggs,
joint author. II. LeButt, Marlene,
joint author. III. Title.
LB1029.G3I53   372.1'3   75-17565
ISBN 0-13-965327-9

Printed in the United States of America.

Inspiration Warrants Recognition.

Dedicated to:

Rosalie Tyner
Sandy Crosser
Don Jones
Jerry and Fran Kilroy
and Brian

ABOUT THE AUTHORS

(left to right, Jones, Ingram, LeButt)

All three authors are experienced elementary teachers in northeastern Ohio. They have served as consultants at area universities, for the International Reading Association Conference, The Ohio Teacher's Association Meetings and at educational seminars. Barbara Ingram is a graduate of Kent State University, Nancy Jones graduated from Bowling Green State University, and Marlene LeButt received her degree from Case Western Reserve University. They are the originators of some of the most effective techniques being used today in the field of Learning Centers via the Workshop method.

0-13-965327

Foreword

The old proverb about the devil finding work for idle hands is outmoded. Today's real problem has to do with idle minds. Children without challenge are bewildered and confused.

It is vitally important that as early as possible, children's interest and enthusiasm be directed to creative learning. They should be encouraged to involve themselves, and their talents, to create the proper environment in which to grow and improve. Ultimately they will be inspired to work in cooperation with their fellow man, to achieve a better life for all. Education is the best medium to attain these desired goals.

In this book the three young authors, who set forth their "Workshop" concept of training, show an unusual understanding of the true purpose of education. The word "education" itself, from the Latin word "educere," signifies a "leading out." That is their stated purpose in advancing this system—to provide the means to draw out from the child's mind the full potential of which he is capable.

They present various ways in which to do this, all predicated on one common denominator—full participation of the child in each shop's operation coupled with his acceptance of responsibility for the results he obtains by his own efforts.

Independence of thought and expression is fostered by giving the student his choice of many projects related to the subject treated in the shop. Games, embodying the principles and basics of the subject matter, have been invented to stimulate and sustain the interest of the participants. Then they are encouraged to proceed to the extent dictated by their own imagination, initiative, and perseverance. Their enthusiasm is amazing and the results often incredible. Children seem to appreciate the fact that information is not just being pounded into their heads, but that they are learning by doing —and having fun in the process.

As, for instance, in the Social Studies Shop, the student elects to pursue the subject of "the United Nations." He may choose to assume the role of a delegate to that body. He does research on the organization, the country he represents, and the customs of its people. His duties as delegate would entail writing letters and reports of his activities to his adopted country, or answering inquiries regarding its mission and stance on issues. Thus the student develops writing skills, facility in speaking, and a knowledge of geography. He acquires a broader horizon through listening to his peers and co-workers presenting different views on the subject—all of which can be useful to him in his future career.

The Creative Writing Shop and Audio Visual Shop offer other examples. Opportunities are afforded the students in this category to present their individual thoughts on various timely topics, via tape and other media that relate to the modern world in which they live. This may take the form of writing plays, poetry, prose, storytelling, broadcasting, all permitting free exercise of their lively imaginations. At the same time it improves their ability to communicate with their fellow students, teachers, and parents, etc., thus building self-confidence and self-respect.

Assignments on a partnership basis in pairs, or a joint venture shared by the groups on bigger projects, teach students the value of team work, and how to get along with other people—a must for successful living.

While the workshop method of teaching offers a multitude of advantages for the students, it is by no means a one-way street. Teachers using the techniques recommended will find it equally rewarding. It will prove an experience interesting beyond their most optimistic expectations.

When they provide the children with the suggestions, tools, and diagrams outlined in the book, and then let their charges express their own natural creativity in translating these ideas into concrete form or action, the resulting responses will be as many and as varied as the personalities of the busy participants. The pride of accomplishment in the beaming faces of the children as they present their finished projects is a joy to see. The satisfaction of helping a child discover latent talent that may some day lead him to prominence in the fields of science, art, literature, or even politics, accrues to the teacher who played a part in his first step in this direction.

So, as we read the book, there emerges a story within a story. If we look between the lines, we see imaginative teachers, dedicated to an all-out effort of turning out well-rounded individuals, going forth equipped first, to think for themselves; second, to cope with the problems of the complex world they will have to live in and lead; and third, to bring a fresh and comprehensive approach to the solutions of their problems.

Madeleine Travis

How This Book Will Help You, the Classroom Teacher—

Each chapter that follows will share with you the results achieved by an advanced form of interest centers which we call our "Workshop." During the day, we schedule time to go to the various shops.

The shops are:

Math Shop
Science Shop
Handart Shop
Reading Shop
Creative Writing Shop
Spelling Shop
A.V. Shop
Social Studies Shop
Health Shop
Language Shop

The "Workshop" concept provides for all the individual differences and needs in *any* classroom, in addition to offering a multitude of possibilities for independent study. One way in which these goals are achieved is through the use of activities on various levels of difficulty in a shop. For example, in the Creative Writing Shop each child has a choice of activities: Report Titles, Story Starters, Titles for a Story, Ideas to Write About, Picture File, Headline File, Pick-a-Story, and Composer's Kit. If a child finds the Headline File too complex, he can choose one of the easier activities such as the Picture File or Composer's Kit.

Another way of achieving these goals is to create shop units consisting of different steps leading to the completion of the unit. These steps may include art activities, a research project, experiments, filmstrips, questions to be answered, models to construct, and so forth. A child should be able to identify with some of these activities. A step that really captures his interest can be further pursued on his own.

Peer learning has an effect on attaining these goals. Whether the shop requires working in partners or alone, when confronted with a problem the child can turn for help to a peer within his group.

We have devoted an entire chapter to each one of the shops, and you will discover how to establish your workshop and keep it running successfully. For each shop you will find a list of all the materials in the shops, an explanation of how to use them, and sample unit ideas. We will explain in practical detail how you can conduct conferences with each child, using the forms we have developed for keeping track of daily and weekly individual progress.

All our concepts are workable ideas and we have tested them all in our classrooms. The shops should be carefully planned and introduced to the children one at a time. Once the packets are made and the materials for shops accumulated, you will be delighted by the atmosphere of eager exploration that prevails.

An important key lies in measuring how much responsibility a child will accept when he is given a chance. Our students have developed an extraordinary ability to take on the responsibilities and work independently. We believe you and your students will achieve the same gratifying sense of satisfaction, excitement, and anticipation from initiating this program and watching it work.

The Authors

Acknowledgments

We would like to recognize the efforts of many who have encouraged us and believed in our book:

Lucile Johnston of Kent State University
Peg Thomas
Mad and Ted Travis
Ann Roman
Jim and Marian Riggs
Martha Lovich
The Second Grade Team: Linda, Sandy, and Kay

Table of Contents

10. Developing Study Units for the Health Shop 169

> List of suggested units of study
> Sample units
> Health Lab
> Board games to make

11. Expressing Yourself Correctly in the Language Shop 187

> Language activities
> Poetry unit
> Card games and board games to make

12. Interest Centers the Workshop Way 212

> Helpful hints
> Ideas for your own workshop
> Culminating activity
> A final word

THE WORKSHOP APPROACH
TO CLASSROOM INTEREST CENTERS:

A Teacher's Handbook
of Learning Games and Activities

Establishing the Model Workshop

The workshop consists of a number of interest centers where children can discover, explore, and develop many concepts. These interest centers are an important part of the daily schedule because they offer an avenue of reaching each child. The activities and games available reinforce the concepts already presented, and provide extended enrichment materials for each individual. With a large assortment of shops, each child is sure to find at least one that he can relate to. The underlying objectives in the formation of a student workshop are developing self-discovery, self-control, responsibility, and leadership qualities in the elementary child.

A teacher can organize a shop pertaining to any subject matter. The shops you include in your workshop will depend upon the needs of the students. Thus, your workshop may differ from year to year. The shops we will describe in detail are the following:

Math Shop
Handart Shop
Science Shop
Reading Shop
Creative Writing Shop
Spelling Shop
Audio Visual Shop
Social Studies Shop
Health Shop
Language Shop

The best way to explain how to set up a workshop is to share our own experiences with you. In order for your workshop to be successful you must open the shops up gradually. The year we began the workshop, with an enrollment of 72 third grade children, we started in September with the Handart Shop and the Reading Shop. In order for both shops to be working at the same time, it was necessary to have pre-workshop instruction where we gave the directions for each shop. During the actual workshop time, we floated among the students answering questions and primarily acting as resource persons. Half of the students worked on handart activities while the other half worked in the Reading Shop. After 30 minutes, the groups changed shops. When the students became accustomed to the procedure (approximately four weeks), we introduced four more shops. Due to this addition, we regrouped the students into six heterogeneous groups. At this point, the students were still changing shops at the end of 30 minutes, visiting two a day. Therefore, it took three days to complete the cycle of six shops. This adjustment took longer, about two months.

Noticing the enthusiasm and self-control the children displayed, we decided to add more shops at the beginning of the new year. At this point in time we have developed the workshop in two different ways: opening four more shops to make ten or opening six more to make twelve. This addition called for regrouping again. The groups will vary in size from 2-3 students to 6 students depending on how many students you have and how many shops you establish. The activities in some shops are conducive to working with partners, such as the Science, Health, and Social Studies Shops. You may want to keep this in mind when organizing your groups.

With ten shops going at one time, we spend one hour and ten minutes for workshop time. The students visit two shops a day for 30 minutes each. It then takes five days to complete the cycle. With 12 shops going, we find it beneficial to extend the workshop time to one hour and forty minutes. The first ten minutes are devoted to pre-workshop instruction. We divide the next hour and a half into 30 minute blocks, allowing the students to visit three shops a day. It now takes them four days to complete the cycle. The remainder of each day is divided into appropriate time blocks for the basic subjects, such as: Reading, Math, Spelling, etc.

SCHEDULING

An orderly workshop requires a system of scheduling. For the child to know exactly what he is doing and when he is doing it we have established a billboard. This billboard is posted in the room for all to see. The stages of the workshop development caused us to make two billboards which will be explained in detail.

The first stage of the workshop consisting of two shops does not require a billboard. The two groups automatically go to both shops every day.

When six shops are involved, the scheduling process is more detailed. In this second stage we constructed a billboard which shows the children at a glance which shops they are to visit that day. With the formation of the six groups we chose one person to pilot each group. The pilot's name identifies his group. The schedule looks like Figure 1-1. The chart is read this way: Neil's group goes to Handart the first half-hour. At the given signal the children change shops. At that time Neil's group exchanges with John's group and proceeds to Reading, while John and his group participate in Handart. Each day we rotate the names of the groups.

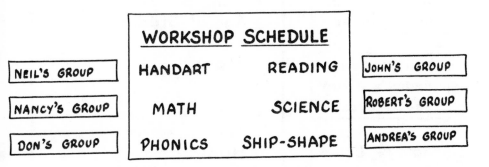

FIGURE 1-1: Workshop Schedule Billboard

In the third stage a new billboard was formed due to the addition of new shops. The billboard for the ten shops would be basically the same as for six shops. Simply add the additional shops and group pilots. Since 12 shops necessitate a more complex method of schedule, the rest of this chapter will be devoted to explaining how that type of workshop is run. Of the 12 shops listed on the billboard shown in Figure 1-2 we will discuss ten in detail in the subsequent chapters. Additional ideas for shops are listed in Chapter 12.

The workshop period is now three 30-minute blocks of time. Let's take a look at the first three groups as an example. On Monday, Neil's group is scheduled for the first 30 minutes at Shop Number 1 (Creative Writing); the second 30 minutes at Shop Number 2 (Spelling); and the third 30 minutes at Shop Number 3 (Science). Terri's group begins at Shop Number 2 (Spelling); the second 30 minutes at Shop Number 3 (Science); and the third 30 minutes at Shop Number 1 (Creative Writing). Jason's group starts at Shop Number 3 (Science); the second 30 minutes at Shop Number 1 (Creative Writing); and the third 30 minutes at Shop Number 2 (Spelling). There are three name

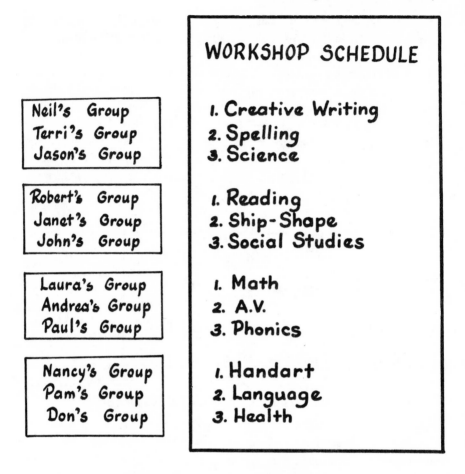

FIGURE 1-2: Second Workshop Billboard

groups on each card. Each day we rotate the name cards down. It takes four days to complete the cycle of all the shops.

For reinforcement of the billboard, every Monday during pre-workshop time we give each pilot a schedule of the group's activities for that week. It is the responsibility of the pilot to inform his group of the contents of the sheet. Figure 1-3 is a sample sheet for Terri's group. Since the workshop cycle takes four days to complete, we excluded Wednesday.

BOOKKEEPING

During the course of the year, our bookkeeping forms kept changing because of the expansion of the workshop. We were constantly striving for simplicity as well as accuracy in our forms. Therefore we have used several.

Terri's Group   **Schedule for week of:** _Jan. 15,_

	SHOPS:	ACTIVITY:
MON.	2. Spelling	Game of your choice
	3. Science	Terri - Becky - Table 1 Marlene - Paul - Table 2
	1. Creat.Writ.	Sign in sheet
TUES.	2. Ship Shape	Heigh in - do exercises
	3. Soc. St.	Continue Soc. St. Lab
	1. Reading	finish reading book - do Riddle Poster.
THURS.	2. A.V.	Finish Scrapbooks
	3. Phonics	Game of your choice
	1. Math	Math Kit - then a game
FRI.	2. Language	Tape + worksheet - then a game of choice
	3. Health	Trace outline of body
	1. Handart	Finish handwriting - start art project.

FIGURE 1-3: Pilot's Schedule for Week

We started out using one form (Figure 1-4) which covers the activities of all the groups for one day. Our second form (Figure 1-5) showed the shops and activities that one group did for the whole week.

The four basic bookkeeping forms we use can be adapted to any shop, depending on how detailed you want your record-keeping to be. We found it necessary to keep bookkeeping records in every shop. In many of our shops we use more than one form in order to have more precise information on each child's performance and progress. We found it convenient to keep a separate folder for each shop with all the bookkeeping forms contained therein.

The first form is a general one in which all the children's names are listed. Space is available for recording the date they visited the shop and comments about the activity done. Figure 1-6 is an example of a form found in the Creative Writing Shop.

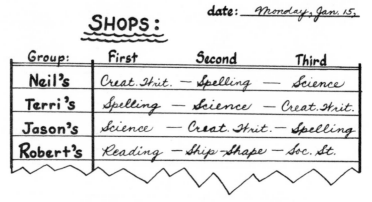

FIGURE 1-4: Sample Daily Schedule

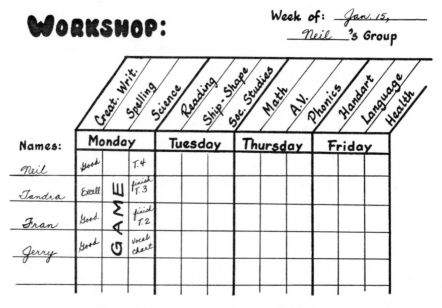

FIGURE 1-5: Sample Weekly Schedule

The second form (Figure 1-7) is slightly different from the first form, although containing the same information. This sample form is from the Science Shop dealing with the unit on Electricity.

The third form (Figure 1-8) is a simpler one which shows at a glance the children's evaluations of the activities completed in the shop. This form is quite effective when used along with Figure 1-7. The sample form shown in Figure 1-8 is from our Handart Shop.

	DATE	ACTIVITY	DATE	ACTIVITY	DATE	ACTIVITY
Mary	9/26	Green card- Lincoln well done				
Bill	9/26	Pink card- -good plot			-finish -very good	
Carol	9/26	Picture Card good			-good -poor, etc.	

FIGURE 1-6: First Basic Bookkeeping Form

Nancy's Group	ELECTRICITY				
	10/25	11/2	11/9	11/16	11/23
Nancy **Don**	finish Table 3	Vocab. Chart Start T. 4	finish T.4	Start T. 1	Start T. 2
Art **Judy**	Start Table 4	Finish T. 4	Do Vocab. Chart	SCIENCE LAB →	
Ann **Dave**	Start T. 1	finish T. 1	Begin T. 2	Finish T. 2	Start T. 3
Bill **Fred**	Start T. 2	Start T. 3	Begin T. 1	Vocab. Chr. Finish T.1	Start T. 4
Pat **Tim**	Vocab. Chart	Start T. 2	finish T. 2	Start T. 3	Start T. 1

FIGURE 1-7: Second Basic Bookkeeping Form

The Creative Writing Shop is a good example of where the fourth form (Figure 1-9) can be used. It is a sign-in sheet where the children write their names next to the activity they choose. This sign-in sheet can be adapted to

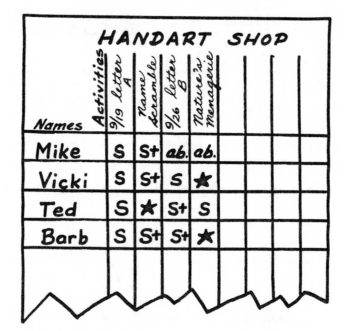

Names	Activities	9/9 letter A	Name scramble	9/26 letter B	Nature's Menagerie			
Mike		S	St	ab.	ab.			
Vicki		S	St	S	★			
Ted		S	★	St	S			
Barb		S	St	St	★			

FIGURE 1-8: Third Basic Bookkeeping Form

SIGN IN PLEASE

Green Card – _____ _____
Orange Card – _____ _____
Pink Card – _____ _____
Yellow Card – _____ _____

Picture Card – _____ _____

Headline Card – _____ _____

Composer's Kit – _____ _____

Pick-a-story – _____ _____

FIGURE 1-9: Fourth Basic Bookkeeping Form

any shop you desire. This form is especially beneficial in the shops where there are numerous games and activities to choose from.

Some shops require specific forms such as the following:

Reading Shop

When a book is taken from the shelf, the child writes the title, the level, and his name on the sign-out sheet shown in Figure 1-10. Individual reading records (Figure 1-11) are kept throughout the year with the following information: date, title of book, activity.

Social Studies, Science, and Health Labs

The bookkeeping in these labs is mainly the responsibility of the children. After working in the lab, they pull their cards and record what they have done for that day. (See Figure 1-12.)

FIGURE 1-10: Reading Shop Sign-out Sheet

PRE-WORKSHOP

Every day we have pre-workshop instruction. Papers that have been checked are passed out and instructions are given. Since each shop involves a unit of study, the instructions will vary anywhere from introducing the unit to reinforcing an activity in the unit, or merely telling the children to proceed with whatever they were working on. If there are no further questions we let the children go by groups to their shops. During the workshop period you will find us giving individual help in all of the areas, checking work that has been completed and answering questions.

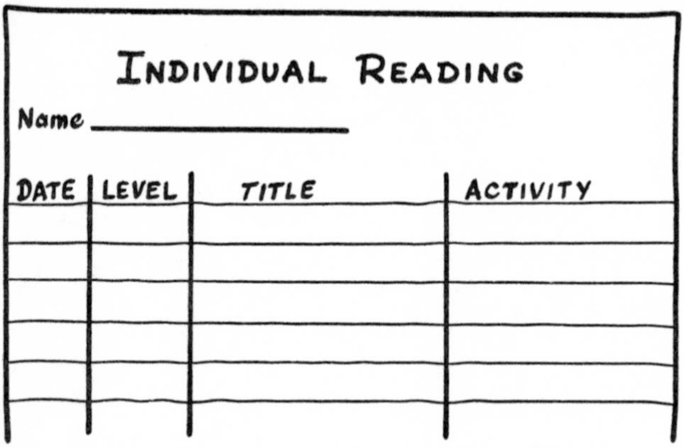

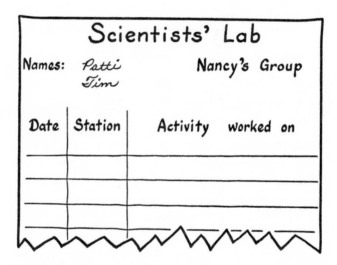

FIGURE 1-11: Individual Reading Record Sheet

FIGURE 1-12: Personal Record Chart for Scientists' Lab

VOLUNTEER AIDES

You may find it beneficial, as we did, to enlist the aid of mothers during workshop. They can be used in any shop. For example, they can sit at the Creative Writing Shop to help the children spell words, or they can be in the Health Shop to help them look up definitions, or at the Science Shop they can help with the experiment. Ideally you can have an aide in each shop. They are very valuable whether they express an interest for one shop or prefer to assist the teacher in floating around the shops.

To show you how our workshop operates, we will take you into our classroom and enable you to experience it through a child's eyes. Neil is one of our students. Through his eyes you will see the 12 shops that are in operation:

IT'S MONDAY MORNING . . .

Neil eagerly checks the Workshop Schedule Billboard to see where his group is scheduled.

"Let's see . . . first I have Creative Writing, then Spelling, and last Science. I think in Creative Writing I'll pick a picture to write about."

Ping . . . ping . . . ping . . . the delightful musical notes of the xylophone chime to summon the children to begin the workshop period. Neil and the other children gather on the floor in the middle of the room for pre-workshop instructions.

At the Creative Writing Shop, Neil learns that they are to begin a new project. "How would you like to write your very own book?" Mrs. Jones asks. She goes on to explain three possibilities . . . an adventure story, a book of poems, or a biography of someone they know.

"Gee, I could write some really neat poems about animals, sports, and maybe even cars!" Neil could hardly wait to get started! He decided on a book of poems.

Ping . . . ping . . . ping . . . 30 minutes later the xylophone chimes the message to change shops. Neil puts his Creative Writing papers in his folder to be checked by Mrs. Jones and proceeds to the Spelling Shop.

"Anyone want to play Scrabble today?" Two children join Neil in word-building as they play the game.

Again 30 minutes later the xylophone chimes. Neil's group goes to the Science Shop. At this time the Science Shop's experiments all deal with electricity. The Science Shop has four tables, each with intriguing problem-solving experiments. Neil and his partner have completed the activities at one of the tables—one was to try to light the miniature light bulb. Today they will learn how to make an electromagnet and how to use it.

ON TUESDAY . . .

Neil heads for the Reading Shop. He's already chosen his book and completed his vocabulary booklet. "All I have to do is get my vocabulary booklet checked by Mrs. Ingram. Then I can get started on one of the other four activities . . . draw a cartoon of my story . . . choose a character from the story to be my friend and write a paragraph telling why . . . make a diorama . . . or choose one of the optional activities."

Thirty minutes later Neil and his group go to the Ship Shape Shop. After weighing in, Neil and his partner do the assigned exercises and mark it on their chart.

The last 30 minutes of the workshop Neil and his group report to the Social Studies Shop. "Last week we found where the equator was on the globe. I wonder what we are going to do today!" When they gathered in their group, Miss LeButt helped them find the latitude and longitude lines on the globe. After all the children in the group found them they played a game with the latitude and longitude lines. Later in the period Miss LeButt suggested three kinds of maps they could make—a neighborhood map, a map of the room, or a school map.

"I think I'll make a map of my neighborhood from home to school." Miss LeButt gave the children the paper to get started.

ON THURSDAY . . .

Neil's group goes to the Math Shop, where one of the activities they work with is a commercially prepared individualized practice kit. The kit contains cards of 20 problems each. According to the number of problems correct, Neil is programmed to go on to the next card. Other mathematics related activities are available.

Neil's second shop of the day is A.V. Some of the children in his group put on earphones and listen to records while others look at filmstrips.

Neil and his group go to the Phonics Shop next. After doing the sheet for that day, the group plays one of the phonics games.

ON FRIDAY . . .

Neil checks the Workshop Schedule again. He sees that his group will go to the Handart Shop. Neil does his handwriting from transparencies of a commercially prepared manual projected on the overhead and then does the art project for that week.

"As soon as I do my handwriting and draw my picture I can get started on our group kite!"

When the xylophone sounds, Neil and his group go to the Language Shop. As Neil passes out the language papers, the rest of the children put the headphones on. "Does everyone have his name on his paper? Is everyone ready to listen to the tape? O.K. I'll start the tape," says Neil. The tape for the week is a detailed explanation of punctuation of friendly letters and instructions on how to do the corresponding paper.

The last shop of the day is Health. "I have already finished my skeleton, the outline of my body, and answered the questions to the filmstrip. There are still some interesting things in my packet—the calcium experiment, vocabulary, backbone experiment, and the test on labeling the bones of the body." Neil works on his calcium experiment.

We have just followed Neil through a typical cycle of our workshop. He has been to all 12 shops and will start at the beginning again with the Creative Writing, Spelling, and Science Shops.

2

Individualizing the Basic Operations Through the Math Shop

The purpose of the Math Shop is twofold. First, it gives the children the much needed drill for the retention of the facts. Second, it offers an array of materials which are a contrast from the flashcard drill and the text. In this chapter we will give you a look at the commercially prepared materials received from school or personal resources and, also, the homemade materials which we prepared.

The basic element in the Math Shop is the individualized math kit which we purchased. As you know, there are many math kits on the market, some of which may suit your needs better than others. The kit we have is composed of 20 sections, each relating to one concept. Within each section the child takes a pre-test which programs him to the various levels he must complete before taking the post-test. Each child has a folder containing the progress chart for the kit. Every time he goes to the Math Shop he does at least two cards, checks his work, and records his progress on the chart.

The rest of the commercially prepared materials are:

multiplication records	beads
walk-on number line	popsicle sticks
flannel board	magnetic numerals
flannel numbers	magnetic discs
flash cards	magnetic math symbols
primary cutouts	abacus
blocks	tangrams

crayon. Since the answers can be found on the back of the sheet, the child then turns the ditto over and checks his work. For convenience, group the sheets in folders according to the process or operation involved.

If there are no extra math dittos available you can make up problems on construction paper and use them in the same manner.

Puzzle Box

The puzzle box provides enjoyment as well as deductive reasoning. The puzzles are filed in a box in folders and numbered consecutively, ranging from simple to complex. Each folder has as many puzzles as there are children in your classroom. The more puzzles you have, the better. We started with 54 and are constantly expanding. The puzzles can be obtained from Math Puzzle books or coloring books, or you can create your own such as the following. The directions for each puzzle are usually included on the puzzle so these can be used independently.

Puzzle #1:   CAN YOU COUNT? (See Figure 2-3.)

Problem 1:   Count the total number of squares you find in this figure.

Problem 2:   This is tricky! How many triangles can you find in this second figure? Make sure you count them all!

Problem 1:

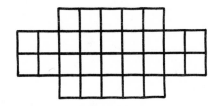

Problem 2:

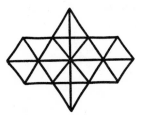

FIGURE 2-3: Math Puzzle #1

Puzzle #2:   CHAIN GAME (See Figure 2-4.)

This is a chain game. Do exactly what it tells you to do, and write that answer in the next open box. See the first example. (The answers that were filled in by the students are underlined.)

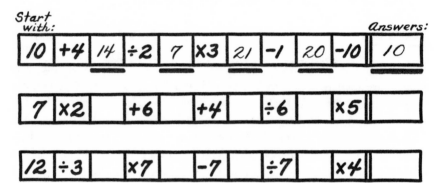

FIGURE 2-4: Math Puzzle #2

Puzzle #3:   STAR WORK (See Figure 2-5.)

Starting with the number in the center of the star, follow the operation indicated using that number and write the final answer in the outside triangle. See the top star for an example.

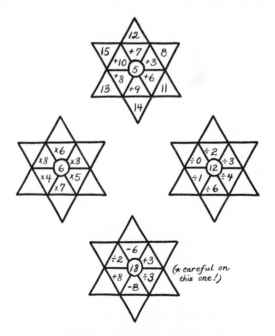

FIGURE 2-5: Math Puzzle #3

Puzzle #4:   HOW MANY? (See Figure 2-6.)

The object of this puzzle is to see how many lost mathematical terms can be found hidden in this array of letters. The words are written horizontally, vertically, and diagonally. Circle all the ones you can find.

FIGURE 2-6: Math Puzzle #4

Puzzle #5:   MATH CROSSWORD PUZZLE (See Figure 2-7.)

Use the following clues to solve this crossword puzzle:

(Across:)

1. 56	3. 9	4. 9	6. 536	9. one thousand,
+56	×10	×8	+261	four hundred and
				twenty.

10. one thousand, five hundred and fifty-six.   12. 6
                                                      × 7

(Down:)

1. 467	2. 136	4. 11	5. 152
−360	+ 83	× 7	+144

7. 300   8. Four thousand, one hundred and fourteen.
  +155

10. 10	11. 8	13. 6
×10	×8	×4

FIGURE 2-7: Math Puzzle #5

Puzzle #6:   ELIMINATION (See Figure 2-8.)

This puzzle is self-explanatory. To solve it, just circle all the problems that are correct.

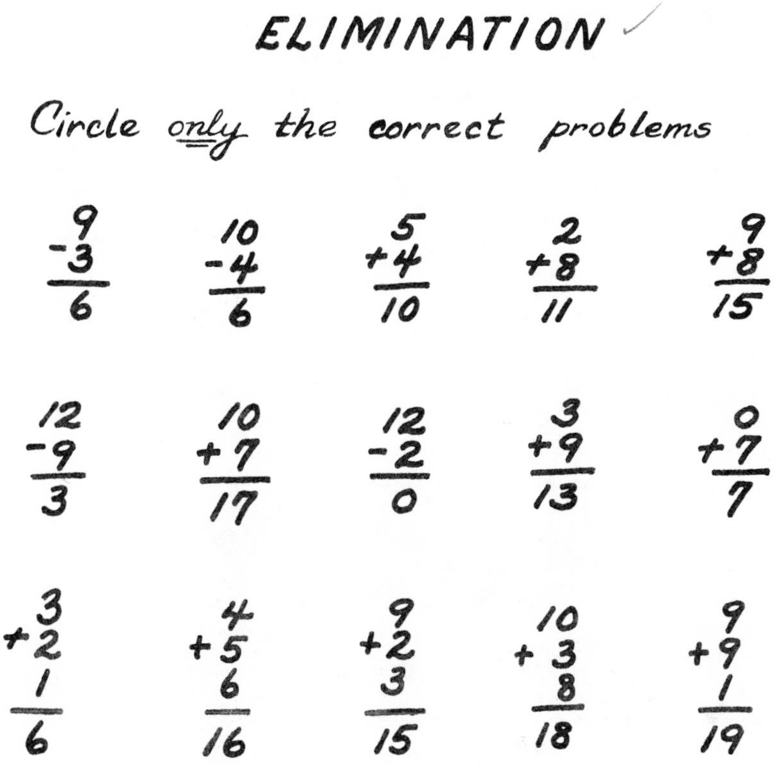

ELIMINATION ✓

Circle only the correct problems

$$\begin{array}{r} 9 \\ -3 \\ \hline 6 \end{array} \qquad \begin{array}{r} 10 \\ -4 \\ \hline 6 \end{array} \qquad \begin{array}{r} 5 \\ +4 \\ \hline 10 \end{array} \qquad \begin{array}{r} 2 \\ +8 \\ \hline 11 \end{array} \qquad \begin{array}{r} 9 \\ +8 \\ \hline 15 \end{array}$$

$$\begin{array}{r} 12 \\ -9 \\ \hline 3 \end{array} \qquad \begin{array}{r} 10 \\ +7 \\ \hline 17 \end{array} \qquad \begin{array}{r} 12 \\ -2 \\ \hline 0 \end{array} \qquad \begin{array}{r} 3 \\ +9 \\ \hline 13 \end{array} \qquad \begin{array}{r} 0 \\ +7 \\ \hline 7 \end{array}$$

$$\begin{array}{r} 3 \\ +2 \\ \hline 1 \\ \hline 6 \end{array} \qquad \begin{array}{r} 4 \\ +5 \\ \hline 6 \\ \hline 16 \end{array} \qquad \begin{array}{r} 9 \\ +2 \\ \hline 3 \\ \hline 15 \end{array} \qquad \begin{array}{r} 10 \\ +3 \\ \hline 8 \\ \hline 18 \end{array} \qquad \begin{array}{r} 9 \\ +9 \\ \hline 1 \\ \hline 19 \end{array}$$

FIGURE 2-8: Math Puzzle #6

Puzzle #7: WHAT ANIMAL CAN MULTIPLY? (See Figure 2-9.)

First, write all the answers to the problems at the top of the puzzle. Next, connect the dots, using the answers from the problems in the order that they appear, to find out what animal can multiply.

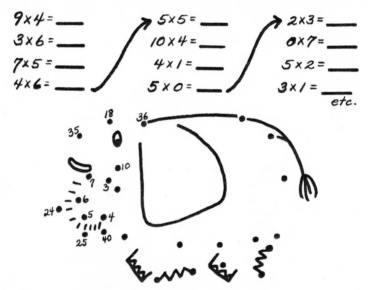

FIGURE 2-9: Math Puzzle #7

MATH PUZZLES

Name: _____

1. Can You Count?
2. Chain Game
3. Star Work
4. How Many?
5. Crossword Puzz.
6. Elimination
7. What Animal Can Multiply?

19. Counting Tree
20. Sum Time
21. Challenge
22.

FIGURE 2-10: Record Chart for Math Puzzles

So that each child can keep a record of what puzzles he has worked on, we have designed the chart shown in Figure 2-10 which he keeps in his folder along with his math kit papers.

Place Value Kit

The Place Value Kit (Figure 2-11) is a device which the children can manipulate to get a better understanding of place value. The materials necessary to make this kit are the following:

6-11" long dowel rod sections
6 wood blocks 4" by 4"
circular wooden discs (approximately 50)
shellac
paint

The circular discs can either be made by a hole saw that fits any standard electric drill or purchased with center holes already in them.

Drill a hole in the center of each wood block large enough to hold a dowel rod securely.

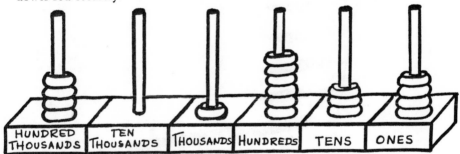

FIGURE 2-11: Place Value Kit

The discs should fit on the dowel rods. Paint the discs bright colors, and then shellac all the discs, dowel rods, and wood blocks. On the front of each block you may want to write one of these titles:

ONES

TENS

HUNDREDS

THOUSANDS

TEN THOUSANDS

HUNDRED THOUSANDS

All of the pieces can be stored in a box. When the child uses the kit, he must set up the blocks in their correct order and then practice either by himself or with others.

Roll-a-Number

Roll-a-Number is a game that the students never seem to get tired of playing. Figure 2-12 shows what our game looks like. The board can be constructed out of plywood or sturdy cardboard and can have as many slots as you desire. The size of your board will depend on the space available in your classroom.

At the back of each slot, write a number. We used the numbers from 0 to 9, the object of the game being to score under 11 or over 21 by rolling three balls. You may want to change those numbers according to your level.

With the back of the board tilted downward, the player uses a soft rubber ball and rolls it down the board three times. He adds up those three numbers, and wins if he has scored under 11 or over 21. The rules may vary if more than one player plays together.

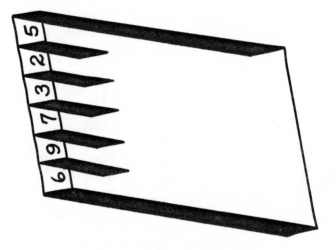

FIGURE 2-12: Roll-a-Number Game

Math Challengers

The Math Challengers provide an opportunity for the students to apply the mathematical skills they have acquired through the various practice materials. One Math Challenger features a story problem to be solved step by step on another sheet of paper. To make one, use a 6″ by 9″ piece of construction paper folded in half. The problem is written on the inside, with the final solution on the back. The cards are numbered on the front cover according to the level of difficulty of the problem. To safeguard the Challengers, it is wise to laminate them.

Electrical Quiz Board

The electrical quiz board (Figure 2-13) is designed as a non-competitive, individual tool which provides matching exercises and drill in the Math Shop. The construction of the board takes a little more elbow grease and time, but the children delight in operating it. This is how you can make your own electrical board:

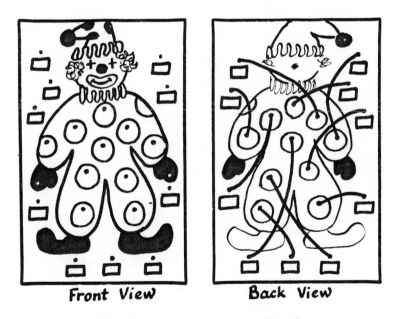

Front View   Back View

FIGURE 2-13: Electric Quiz Board

Materials needed:

piece of plywood
covered wire
screws and bolts
paint
6-volt battery
6-volt light bulb
1 flashlight reflector head

Steps in construction:

1. Determine the size you want your board to be.
2. Sketch the design you want on your board. It can be designed as a figure or as a column of questions and answers. (In the figure, the questions can be inside and the answers outside, as shown in the illustration.)
3. Establish the size of the problem cards and answer cards to be used on the board. Decide how many you want and where you want them placed. A standard size would serve best, as you will probably be changing the cards often when changing operations.
4. Set screws and bolts in place according to predetermined electrical circuits—one screw for each question and one for each answer.*
5. Run electrical wire (on the back of board) connecting the screw of one question to an answer.
6. Drill a hole large enough for the small flashlight reflector head to go through—in place of the nose.
7. Paint the board.
8. Attach the flashlight reflector and bulb.
9. Write the problems and answers on tags and attach to appropriate screws.
10. Attach battery and stand to the back of the board.
11. Place two wires on the 6-volt battery, one wire on the positive post and one on the negative post. The wire on the positive post is the clown's one arm and will be used to play the game. The wire on the negative post will run to the flashlight reflector and serve as a ground.
12. Attach a wire to the end of the flashlight (6-volt) bulb. This wire is the clown's other arm.

*Since the children may begin to learn which two screws are connected, you may want to rewire the screws often.

To play the game:

Select a problem within the clown. Touch one of the clown's arms to the metal screw at the top of this problem. Select on the outside of the clown the answer you think is correct for the problem, and touch the other arm of the clown to the screw. If you have chosen the correct answer, the circuit will be completed, and the clown's nose will light up.

HOMEMADE GAMES

Fraction Fantasy

Materials needed:

construction paper
20″ by 30″ poster board
4 one-inch painted dowel rods for tokens
1 painted cube

Making the game board:

Using six different colors of construction paper, cut out forty 2″ circles. Starting at the lower left hand corner (see Figure 2-14), make a winding path to the upper right hand corner of the board, leaving an empty space approximately 12½″ high and 9″ wide in the lower right hand corner. In this empty space mount five 4 ″ by 4 ″ squares and number them consecutively. In the upper right hand corner place a castle indicating the finish line. In three of the circles write "Take another turn" and in three others write "Miss one turn."

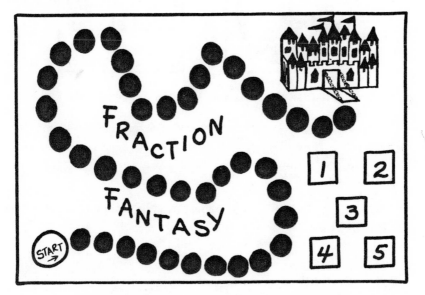

FIGURE 2-14: Fraction Fantasy Game Board

Making the tokens and cube:

Paint the four dowel rods four different colors. Write 1, 2, 3, 4, 5, or "any number," on the painted cube.

Making the game cards:

This game will have five sets of 3″ by 3″ cards, each dealing with one phase of the study of fractions. The first set of 3″ by 3″ cards consists of sectioned circles and rods. (See Figure 2-15 for an example.)

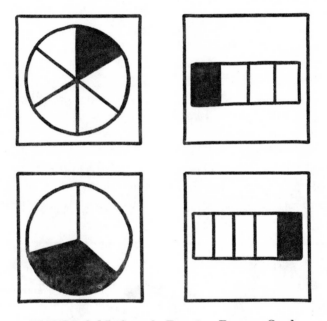

FIGURE 2-15: Sample Fraction Fantasy Cards

The second set of 3″ by 3″ cards will have fractional problems such as these:

$$\frac{1}{4} \text{ of } 36 \qquad \frac{1}{2} \text{ of } 2 \qquad \frac{1}{3} \text{ of } 27 \qquad \frac{1}{8} \text{ of } 64$$

The third set of 3″ by 3″ cards contains additional problems of common fractions like these:

$$\frac{2}{5}+\frac{2}{5} \qquad \frac{3}{6}+\frac{2}{6} \qquad \frac{2}{7}+\frac{1}{7} \qquad \frac{3}{8}+\frac{5}{8}$$

The fourth set of 3″ by 3″ cards contains number lines divided into sections labeled **M**. An example of this is:

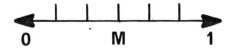

The fifth set of cards gives two fractions with a circle between them, like these:

$$\frac{1}{5} \circ \frac{2}{10} \qquad\qquad \frac{1}{2} \circ \frac{5}{8} \qquad\qquad \frac{1}{4} \circ \frac{1}{8}$$

Playing the game:

Shuffle the five sets of cards separately and place them face down in the respective squares on the game board. Place all the players' tokens on *start*.

The first player rolls the cube to see what number set card he must draw. If the player rolls a number he draws a card from that numbered pile and states his answer.

For Card Set #1 the players must give the fractional number of the colored area shown in the circle or the rod.

For Card Set #2 the players must read the fractional problem, divide it and give the answer.

For Card Set #3 the players read the fractional addition problem and give the answer.

For Card Set #4 the players name the fraction represented by the letter M on the number lines.

For Card Set #5 the players read the fractional phrase and state whether the fractions are greater than, less than, or equal to, in place of the circle.

When the player gives the correct answer he is allowed to move the number of spaces designated on the cube and the card set. If his answer is wrong he does not move. Play continues in this manner until the player who reaches the castle first is declared the winner.

Measurement Magician

Materials needed:

20″ by 30″ poster board
construction paper
4 one-inch painted dowel rods for tokens
1 painted cube numbered 1, 2, 3, 1, 2, 3.

Making the game board:

To the right of the poster board draw a magician with a wand in his hand. Write the title, "Measurement Magician," above the picture. Place four wand paths with their four starting positions on the left side of the board. The four wand paths should end before the magician picture. Each wand path is divided into 12 sections. See Figure 2-16 for an illustration of the final product.

FIGURE 2-16: Measurement Magician Game Board

Making the cards:

Rule off the cards into 2″ by 2″ squares. On each card write problems that will require the players to change from one unit of measurement to another unit. Some examples that would be found on the cards are:

4 feet = _____ inches	2 yards = _____ feet
2 quarts = _____ cups	3 gallons = _____ quarts
2 feet 3 inches = _____ inches	

Number the cards so that an answer booklet can be made.

How to play the game:

Each player puts his token on his own starting position. The object of the game is for a player to get to the opposite end of his wand first. The first player draws a card and reads the problem. He figures out the answer to the problem. He then reads the whole problem again, filling in the blank with his answer. The player to his right finds the number card in the answer booklet and checks to see if the first player is correct. If the first player gave the right answer he is allowed to roll the cube and move that number of spaces on his wand. If his answer is incorrect he is not permitted to roll the cube. The play of the game continues until a player reaches the end of his wand first and is declared the winner.

Math Scrabble

Materials needed:

14" by 14" poster board
2 ditto masters
construction paper
1 painted cube with sides numbered 0, 1, 2, 3, 4, 5.

To make the game board:

Leaving a ½" margin on all edges of the board, rule off the playing area into 1" squares. You should have 13 squares both across and down, with a total of 169 squares. In the squares across the top of the board, starting in the top left square, fill in each consecutive square with the following symbols and numerals: the multiplication sign (X), 1, 2, 3, 4, 5, 6, 7, 8, 9, 10, 11, and 12. In the first column down the left edge of the playing area, you will already have the multiplication sign in the top box, so number the rest of the squares in that column from 1 to 12 inclusively. The complete board should look like an enlarged, empty multiplication table, as that is exactly what it will be used for.

Variation: To add a challenge to the game, you may want to make another table on the reverse side of the board, using the same numbers but scrambling their order.

To make the game cards:

These are not cards, but simply 1" squares with numbers on them that fit on the game board. To make these "cards," rule off the two ditto masters into 1" squares. In each of these squares write the following numerals the number of times specified:

Numeral	Amount of Cards	Numeral	Amount of Cards
1	one	2	two
3	two	4	three
5	two	6	four
7	two	8	four
9	three	10	four
11	two	12	six
14	two	15	two
16	three	18	four
20	four	21	two
22	two	24	six
25	one	27	two
28	two	30	four
32	two	33	two
35	two	36	five
40	four	42	two
44	two	45	two
48	four	49	one
50	two	54	two
55	two	56	two
60	four	63	two
64	one	66	two
70	two	72	four
77	two	80	two
81	one	84	two
88	two	90	two
96	two	99	two
100	one	108	two
110	two	120	two
121	one	132	two
144	one		

Run off four copies of each ditto on four different colors of construction paper. This will give you four different sets of the above.

How to play the game:

Each player starts with his own colored set of number cards. He rolls the cube to see how many of his cards he may place on the board. If he rolls a 5, he may place 5 of his numbered cards on the appropriate square on the board. If he rolls a 0, he may not play any of his cards. When the board is completely filled, the players count the number of cards they have on the board and the player who has the most wins the game.

Blitz

Materials needed:

20" by 20" poster board
construction paper
4 painted tokens
1 cube numbered 0, 1, 2, 3, 4, 5.
approximately 7" by 7" picture of a town or a city of buildings

How to make the game board:

After covering the board with brown construction paper, mount the picture of the city in the center of the board. In each of the four corners mount a black round circle. From each of these circles, arrange some gray 1"-wide strips of construction paper leading from the circles to the city. (See Figure 2-17 for one possible arrangement.) Then divide the strips into 1" blocks. In one place on the board, mount a brightly colored 3" by 3½" piece of construction paper.

How to make the playing cards:

Rule off about fifty 2½" by 3" blocks on some construction paper that matches the 3" by 3½" block mounted on the board. In each of these sections, write a multiplication problem or any other operation you wish to stress.

FIGURE 2-17: Blitz Game Board

How to play the game:

Each player places his token on a black circle that represents his foxhole, the beginning of his tunnel to the city. In turn, each player chooses a playing card, reads the problem, and tells the answer aloud. If his answer is correct, he may roll the cube to see how far through his tunnel he may move. If he answers incorrectly, he does not move. The first player to "blitz" the city and capture it is the winner of the game.

A *variation:* After the players capture the city, give them a different set of cards, such as division, and have them return to their foxhole to win the game.

Disneyland Dream

Materials needed:

20″ by 20″ poster board
construction paper
4 painted tokens
1 cube numbered 0 through 5

FIGURE 2-18: Disneyland Dream Game Board

How to make the game board:

In the center of the board, draw the outline of a large, puffy cloud that practically covers the entire board. In the bottom left corner, outside this cloud, draw a person sleeping with the cloud representing his dream. (See Figure 2-18.)

In the top right corner, outside the cloud, mount a bright yellow sun. Inside the sun write "Wake up."

Out of different colors of construction paper cut smaller clouds approximately 2″ in diameter. You may need as many as 30 of these. Arrange them inside the large cloud as a winding path from the sleeping person to the sun. In the space not filled in the cloud, you may want to draw or cut out some Disneyland characters and mount them in various places, along with the title of the board, and a 3″ by 3″ orange square labeled "DD cards."

How to make the playing cards:

Rule off five sheets of orange construction paper into 3″ by 3″ blocks. Inside each of these blocks, write a brief story problem that is suitable for your grade level. Number each card in one of the corners.

How to make the answer booklet:

The booklet is made of pieces of construction paper sandwiched between two pieces of cardboard. The answers inside are numbered according to the numbers found in the corners of the playing cards.

How to play the game:

Players start where the person is sleeping, and try to be the first to travel through this Disneyland Dreamland and "wake up." Each player in turn draws a playing card, reads the problem aloud, solves it either mentally or on paper, and then tells his answer to the other players. While he is still figuring out the problem, however, one of the others must look up the answer in the booklet. If the player answers correctly, he may roll the cube and move his token. Play continues until one of the players "wakes up" and wins the game.

Sunken Treasure

Materials needed:

15″ by 18″ poster board
4 colored tokens
2 cubes, each numbered 1 through 6.

How to make the game board:

Cover the bottom 4/5 of the board with blue construction paper. On the top, above the blue area, draw a picture of the bottom of a boat with a ladder extending into the water. The spaces of the ladder are the starting positions for the players. From the ladder, add 1″ squares that would make a path through the blue water and end at a "sunken treasure." (See Figure 2-19.)

How to play the game:

Each player places his token on a space of the ladder, and rolls the cubes. If the sum total of the numbers rolled is an even number, the player may move *forward* that many spaces. If the sum total of the numbers rolled is an odd number, the player must move *backward* that many spaces. When moving backward, a player may sometimes go back as far as the ladder; then if he again rolls an odd number, he does not move, but has to wait until he rolls an even number. The first player to reach the "sunken treasure" is the winner.

FIGURE 2-19: Sunken Treasure Game Board

3

Combining Penmanship and Creative Artistry in the Handart Shop

The Handart Shop is a blend of handwriting and art activities. The assignment in the Handart Shop is to complete the handwriting first and then do the art project.

HANDWRITING

To take the boredom out of handwriting we use riddles. We try to find a riddle in which the letter the students are practicing appears frequently. The procedure for using the riddle activity is as follows:

1) Practice writing the letter.
2) Practice words from the riddle that contain the letter.
3) Write the riddle.
4) Draw a picture illustrating the riddle.

To assist you in finding a riddle for each letter, here are some suggestions:

RIDDLES

A— If an athlete gets athlete's foot, what does an astronaut get?   (Missle-toe.)

B— Why is Bobby's nose not 12 inches long?   (Because it would then be a foot.)

C— What comes out of a burning forest?   (Crispy Critters.)

D— What did you use yesterday, but made today?   (Your bed.)

E— When are cooks cruel?   (When they beat the eggs and whip the cream.)

F— How did the firefly feel when he flew into the fan?   (De-lighted, of course.)

G— Which is bigger, Mr. Bigger or Mr. Bigger's baby?   (The baby; he's a little bigger.)

H— Why is your hand like a hardware store?   (Because it has hard nails.)

I— What is the highest public building in your city?   (The library; it has many stories.)

J— When was beef the highest it has ever been?   (When Jersey, the cow, jumped over the moon.)

K— Why did Farmer Jack name is pink pig "Ink"?   (Because it kept running out of its pen.)

L— What is the longest word in the English language?   (*SMILES*. There's a *mile* between the first *s* and the last *s*.)

M— What's Smokey the Bear's middle name?   ("The.")

N— Three men were under one umbrella but none of them got wet. Why?   (Because it wasn't raining.)

O— What do you take off the floor before you go to bed?   (Your feet.)

P— How can a person communicate with Peppy the fish?   (By dropping him a line.)

Q— What is the difference between Queenie the ballet dancer and a quacking duck? (One goes quick on her legs and the other goes quack on her legs.)

R— How do you stop a herd of elephants from charging?   (You take away their credit cards.)

S— What happens when you eat yeast and drink shoe polish?   (You rise and shine.)

T— What begins with "T" and ends with "T" and has "T" inside? (A teapot.)

U— Up and down, up and down, touching neither sky nor ground. What am I? (A pump handle.)

V— What inventions have helped men get up in the world?   (The elevator and the alarm clock.)

W— What is black and white, black and white, black and white, and black and white?   (A black and white penguin rolling down the stairs.)

X— What might the tailpipe on Joe's taxi say to the tailpipe on Rex's taxi as they exit off the expressway?   (Boy, am I exhausted!)

Y— What is yours and used by everybody else more than yourself? (Your name.)

Z— Why did the zebra want a zipper on his zoo cage door?   (He wanted to ZIP in and out.)

A variation from the riddles is the use of stories and poems. The long stories and poems are broken up into paragraphs and verses, thus enabling the poem or story to extend over a period of time. For each part the child draws his own corresponding picture. When the poem or story is completed the student can compile his own book from the handwriting assignments. Student books can also be assembled using the riddles and jokes.

TITLES OF STORIES

Aesop's Fairy Tales such as:

The Wind and the Sun	The Grasshopper and the Ants
A Lion and a Mouse	The Town Mouse and the Country
The Fox and the Crow	Mouse

The Shepherd's Boy and the Wolf

Grimm's Fairy Tales such as:

The Elves and the Shoemaker	Rumpelstiltskin
Rapunzel	The Golden Goose

Hansel and Gretel

Hans Christian Andersen's Fairy Tales such as:

The Ugly Duckling	The Tinder Box
The Real Princess	Five Peas in a Pod

The Angel

English Folk Tales such as:

Henny Penny	Teeny Tiny
Johnny Cake	The Story of the Three Pigs

The Old Woman and the Pig

TITLES OF POEMS

A Visit from St. Nicholas—Clement Clarke Moore
The Little Land—Robert Louis Stevenson
My Shadow—Robert Louis Stevenson
Allie—Robert Graves
Sounds in the Morning—Eleanor Farjeon
Market Square—A.A. Milne
The Cave Boy—Laura E. Richards
Wynken, Blynken, and Nod—Eugene Field

Thanksgiving Day—Lydia Maria Child
Hiding—Dorothy Aldis
Godfrey Gordon Gustavus Gore—William Brighty Rands
The Walrus and the Carpenter—Lewis Carroll
Tale of Custard the Dragon—Ogden Nash
How to Tell the Wild Animals—Carolyn Wells
The Elf and the Dormouse—Oliver Herford
The Owl and the Pussycat—Edward Lear
The Spider and the Fly—Mary Howitt
Little Orphan Annie—James Whitcomb Riley
The Sugarplum Tree—Eugene Field
Nonsense Alphabet—Edward Lear
The Duel—Eugene Field
Animal Crackers—Christopher Morley
The Children's Hour—Henry Wadsworth Longfellow

We have found that a convenient method of displaying the handwriting lesson is to use the overhead projector. This enables the teacher to prepare in advance all the transparancies for each handwriting unit.

ART

The art area of the Handart Shop always has an abundance of materials readily accessible. A suggested list of everyday materials is as follows:

construction paper of various sizes and colors	clay
newsprint	glue
tracing paper	scissors
graph paper	magic markers
paints	glitter
brushes	crayons
watercolors	colored chalk
fingerpaint	wood blocks
foil	paper plates
wax paper	paper cups
newspaper	straws
magazines	bottle caps
material	paper bags
yarn	tin cups
macaroni	Styrofoam egg cartons

All these supplies are kept in a cupboard, and usually the children are responsible for keeping it orderly. When the children want to use these supplies for a project, they work at the art table in the art "studio."

ART PROJECTS

When it comes to art, each child has his own style and imagination. Our projects are all geared towards each child's own type of originality. This is accomplished by giving a minimum of directions and by offering a wide range of media.

SEPTEMBER ART

Name Scramble (Figure 3-1)

FIGURE 3-1: Name Scramble

Materials needed:

set of 2″ stenciled letters
9 ″× 12 ″ construction paper
pencils, glue, scissors
1″-wide strips for border

Procedure:

1. Decide which name you want to use—first or last.
2. Select two complementary colors of construction paper.
3. Trace and cut out all letters on one of the sheets.
4. Arrange the letters in a visually pleasing design on the second sheet.
5. Glue them.
6. Add the 1″ strips (same color as the letters) as a border or frame.

Nature's Menagerie (Figure 3-2)

Materials needed:

lid of a box
assortment of small twigs, beans, leaves, stones, weeds, etc.
Saran Wrap
paint, glue, yarn, masking tape, hole punch
clear acrylic spray

FIGURE 3-2: Nature's Menagerie

Procedure:

1. Determine whether you want the lid to hang vertically or horizontally.
2. Punch a hole on each side in the upper corner on the lip of the lid for hanging purposes.
3. Paint the entire lid.
4. Arrange the twigs, leaves, beans, stones, weeds, etc. to form a nature scene.
5. Glue them in place.
6. Thread the yarn through one hole, taking it inside the lid and out the other hole. Tie the ends in a knot or bow, thus making a hanger for your Nature's Menagerie.
7. To protect the scenes, spray with a clear acrylic or plastic-type spray.
8. Cover the entire lid with Saran Wrap, pull it tight, and then secure it in the back with masking tape.

OCTOBER ART

Flying Halloweeners (Figure 3-3)

Materials needed:

18″ x 24″ white drawing paper
yarn, crayons, glue, hole punch

FIGURE 3-3: Flying Halloweeners

Procedure:

1. Cut the paper into 9 "× 24 " pieces.
2. Draw and color your Haloween scene on the strip horizontally.
3. Fold the paper into thirds. Then glue the ends together.
4. Punch a hole in the middle of each side at the top.
5. Attach three strands of yarn and hang from the ceiling.

Create-a-Creature

Materials needed:

newspaper
clay
name tags

Procedure:

1. Cover the studio table with newspaper.
2. *Assignment:* Design a creature that does not resemble anything you have ever seen.
3. Make up an original name for it and write it on the name tag.
4. Display the creatures.

5. *Follow-up:* Write a story about your creature, including details about where he came from, his needs for survival, etc.

NOVEMBER ART

Puzzle Pack

Materials needed:

drawing paper
paint, glue, scissors, ruler, shellac
magazines
cardboard

The pack consists of two kinds of puzzles, one making your own picture and one using magazines.

Procedure:

1. Make sure the cardboard is the same size as the drawing paper.
2. Draw and paint a picture on the paper.
3. Glue the paper to the cardboard.
4. Cut the cardboard into various shapes to produce puzzle pieces.
5. Shellac each piece entirely—front, back, and edges.
6. Follow the same steps using a magazine picture (eliminating Step 2).
7. Each puzzle can be stored in an envelope.
8. *Follow-up:* Exchange puzzles with classmates.

Thanksgiving Murals

Materials needed:

3 sheets of mural paper 6' long
crayons, newsprint

Procedure:

1. One mural will depict the first Thanksgiving scene.
2. The second mural will represent the Thanksgiving of today.
3. The last mural will portray the Thanksgiving of the future.
4. Before the students start each mural, they must decide the important things that must be included in their scene. Then they practice drawing them on newsprint.
5. The background is just as important as the objects in the mural. Each mural background should show the appropriate era.

DECEMBER ART

Place Mats and Napkin Rings (Figure 3-4)

Materials needed:

assorted construction paper
12 "× 18 " colored oaktag
newsprint, magic markers, scissors, glue
cardboard tubes
acrylic polymer and brushes, shellac thinner

FIGURE 3-4: Place Mats and Napkin Rings

Procedure:

Place Mats

1. Decide on the subject matter of your place mat; for example: watermelon, flower, strawberry, butterfly, sun, dog, turtle.
2. Practice drawing the chosen object on newsprint, making sure it covers most of the paper.
3. Draw the desired shape on the four sheets of oaktag and cut them out.
4. Using construction paper and magic markers, fill in the details of your object.
5. To protect the mats, use the acrylic polymer or shellac, giving the mat at least one good coat.

Napkin Rings

1. Cut the tubes from any paper product into 1½" segments.
2. Cover them with construction paper.

3. Decorate the napkin rings by one of the two methods shown in Figure 3-4.
4. Shellac or polymer the napkin rings.

Stencil Christmas Cards

Materials needed:

clay, tempera paint, liquid detergent
4" printing roller
carving tools: butter knives, forks, paint brushes
Styrofoam meat or egg trays
newsprint, newspapers
construction paper

Procedure:

1. Cut the construction paper in various sizes which when folded can make greeting cards.
2. Prepare the paint by mixing equal amounts of paint and liquid detergent.
3. On newsprint, design your own *simple* Christmas card.
4. Transfer this design to the back side of the Styrofoam tray (not the inside) or to the chunk of clay (about 3"× 3" and 2" thick).
5. With the end of a brush, press carefully to make an indent in the surface.

   (*REMEMBER*—the part of your design that you push in *will not print*.)

6. Different objects may be used in the clay for texture—forks, hair pins, pencil erasers, etc.
7. To apply the paint, simply roll the roller in the paint and then on your "print." Or you can roll the paint out on a piece of wax paper, and press the print in this.
8. *To print:* Place the print where you want it on the front of your card and press firmly.
9. Remove your print carefully.
10. You can make many cards from this same print, using different colors of construction paper and paint.

JANUARY ART

Computer Inventions

Materials needed:

12"× 18" white drawing paper

ruler, glue, black crayon
aluminum foil, washers, nuts, yarn, bottle caps, material, etc.

Procedure:

1. Invent your own computer, using a ruler when necessary for the straight lines.
2. With the black crayon, outline any lines of the computer you desire.
3. Using the other materials you want, finish the computer.
4. *Follow-up:* Give your computer a name and tell what it is used for.

Scratch Board

Materials needed:

9" by 12" white drawing paper
crayons, scissors
black paint, liquid detergent, paint brushes
newspapers

Procedure:

1. Fill in the whole drawing paper with little patches of color, using the crayons and pressing hard.
2. Mix a very small amount of liquid detergent with the black paint.
3. Cover the entire drawing paper with the black paint mixture.
4. Allow to dry completely.
5. Using one blade of the scissors, scratch out a picture.

FEBRUARY ART

Milk Chalk Flags

Materials needed:

old sheets or material
instant powdered milk
colored chalk
water
big container (approximately 1-gallon size)
stick big enough for each flag

Procedure:

1. In keeping with a patriotic theme, design a flag that you would want to represent your country.

2. Cut the material to the size you want your flag to be.
3. Mix 1 1/3 cup powdered milk and 3 3/4 cup water in the big container.
4. Dip each flag into this mixture and squeeze out the excess.
5. While the material is still wet, lay it out on a flat surface and draw your flag, using the colored chalk.
6. When it's almost dry, put it between two sheets of manila paper and iron it.
7. Staple or glue your flag to the stick.
8. This never smears and has much body, but is NOT WASHABLE.

Mini-Love Plaques (Figure 3-5)

Materials needed:

watercolors
India ink and pens
typing paper or duplicating paper
a piece of wood
shellac and shellac thinner, brushes
masking tape and yarn for hanger

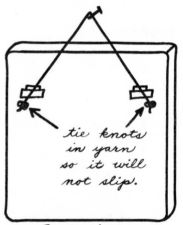

tie knots in yarn so it will not slip.

Back view

FIGURE 3-5: Mini Love Plaque

Procedure:

1. Sand your piece of wood, smoothing out all corners and edges—sanding *with* the grain of the wood.
2. Brush the entire piece with a watercolor, diluting your color so it appears stained and not painted.
3. Outline your piece of wood on typing paper. Sketch your picture dealing with love inside this outline, making sure you leave a border on all four sides.
4. Using watercolors, paint over the sketch, blending the colors together. For example, if your sketch includes a tree and a lake, apply a patch of green watercolor in the general area of the tree, blending towards the patch of blue in the general vicinity of the lake.
5. Allow this to dry thoroughly.
6. With India ink, outline your sketch and add any extra details.
7. Allow this to dry thoroughly.
8. Cut out your picture in any shape.

9. Shellac your board, and while it is still wet mount your picture in the middle of the board, pressing out any air bubbles.
10. Add another coat of shellac to the entire plaque.
11. To hang see illustration in Figure 3-5.

MARCH ART

Kites

Materials needed:

2 sticks, 24" long and 36" long
tissue paper
rubber cement
string, cloth
paints, scissors
paper reinforcements

Procedure:

1. Find the middle of the 24" stick and measure 12" down on the 36" stick. Cross the sticks on this mark and tie them together.
2. Make a groove at each end of the sticks.
3. Run string around the outside of the kite in the grooves.
4. Pull the string firmly and tie the ends together.
5. Place the kite frame on tissue paper and trace around it 1" larger than the kite frame.
6. Cut it out.
7. Design the picture you want on the kite and paint it.
8. After it is dry, place it face down with the kite frame on top of it.
9. Put rubber cement on the extra inch border and fold it up over the string.
10. Tie a length of string from one end of the 24" stick to the other end on the back side of the kite, pulling taut to form a pocket in the kite.
11. Measure 8" from each end of the 36" stick. Make a small hole here through the paper at each end.
12. Put round paper reinforcements on both sides of the holes.
13. Through the top hole and around the stick attach one end of a 28" length of string. Attach the other end of string through the other hole in the same way. Thus, the string hangs on the painted side of the kite.
14. Tie kite cord to this string with a slip knot.
15. Make a tail for your kite and attach.

Finger Print Art

Materials needed:

colored construction paper
fingerpaint

Procedure:

1. Plan a picture with any March theme.
2. Use fingerpaint on your fingertips to paint the picture. There are two things you must remember: (1) Use only one finger at a time. (2) Put only a little bit of paint on your fingertip so the impression of your fingertip will show through.
3. Your painting will be a series of finger*prints*, not a smearing of fingerpaint.

APRIL ART

Egg-Coloring Designs (Figure 3-6)

Materials needed:

12″ by 18″ drawing paper
crayons, paints, scissors

FIGURE 3-6: Easter Egg Design

Procedure:

1. Make a pile of large and medium eggs on the paper.
2. Design each of the Easter eggs.
3. Color the Easter eggs, pressing the crayon firmly.
4. Prepare cups of watered-down pastel tempera paints. Use two parts white to one part red, blue, green, orange, yellow, etc. Add water to make it thinner.
5. Use the pastel color of your choice, paint over the entire picture.
6. Frame the picture if desired.

Papier-Mache Easter Baskets (Figure 3-7)

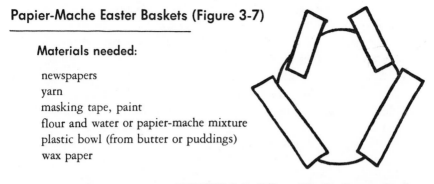

Materials needed:

newspapers
yarn
masking tape, paint
flour and water or papier-mache mixture
plastic bowl (from butter or puddings)
wax paper

FIGURE 3-7: Papier-Mache Bunny Baskets

Preparation:

1. For your convenience, you may want to prepare some of the pieces before starting the project. The pieces needed are:

> EARS—Roll a half-sheet of newspaper to make a flat 1½" wide strip. Fold in a U shape, and trim the ends to come to a point. This is later taped to the head as ears.
>
> HEAD—The head is an oval-shaped ball of newspaper.
>
> LEGS—To make one leg, use one sheet of newspaper, folded in half, and then fold as you did the ears. Fold this long strip into thirds and tape together. (This should be about 1" thick and about 3"-4" long.) You will need four legs for each basket.
>
> BODY—A whole sheet of newspaper wrinkled slightly in a long roll.

2. Place wax paper on the table where you plan to work.
3. Prepare the papier-mache mixture. When using flour and water, mix to the consistency of a thick paste.
4. Cut hundreds of newspaper strips. A good workable size is 8" by 1¼".

Procedure:

1. Start with plastic bowl right side up on the paper. Wrap the wrinkled newspaper around the base of the bowl.
2. Dunk paper strips in the mache mixture, clean off the excess paste, then cover the bowl and newspaper with these strips.
3. Turn the form over and tape the four legs on as shown in Figure 3-8. Then cover with papier-mache strips. Let this much dry.
4. Place the body on its feet and tape the head in place. Cover with mache strips.
5. Put the ears on and cover with mache strips to keep them in place.

6. Cover the completed basket with one more layer of strips, then let it dry.
7. When dry, paint it.
8. Paint facial details on, and add whiskers with construction paper.
9. Glue on a yarn ball for the tail.
    a. Wrap yarn around a 3″ wide piece of cardboard. The more times it is wrapped around, the fuller the ball.
    b. Slide the yarn off the cardboard and tie it in the middle with a piece of yarn.
    c. Cut the loops at each end and fluff into a ball.

FIGURE 3-8: Finished Bunny Basket

MAY ART

Rock and Board Artistry

Materials needed:

rocks, wood scraps
paint, polymer acrylic

Rock Artistry

Procedure:

1. Paint the rock. Allow to dry.

2. On the top of the rock paint a flower or design. When using more than one color, allow each color to dry before going on to the next color.
3. Put one coat of polymer acrylic on the completed rock.

Board Artistry

Procedure:

1. Paint the board. Allow to dry.
2. Choose a magazine picture to place on the wood.
3. Center the picture on the wood and glue in place.
4. Put one coat of polymer acrylic over the entire wood picture.

Candlesticks

Materials needed:

glass jars with lids
glue, paint
small stones

Procedure:

1. Collect various shapes of glass jars with lids. (No labels or lettering on the jars.)
2. Place the jars one on top of another, making the shape of the candlestick that you like and making it as tall as you want.
3. After deciding how you want the jars, put small stones in the bottom jar to weight it down.
4. At the top of the candlestick use an upside-down jar lid for the place where the candle will sit.
5. Glue the jars together.
6. Paint the candlestick.

4

Self-Discovery in the Science Shop

The goal of our Science Shop is to encourage the development of children's scientific nature through their own informal investigation. We do not use texts in presenting scientific concepts; rather the children learn by the experimental approach.

DESCRIPTION OF THE SCIENCE SHOP

Four tables make up the physical environment of the Shop. Each table is labeled numerically with a colorful sign. One concept or unit of study is presented through the use of all four tables. Four different experiments or activities, one at each table, are used to reinforce the concept.

There may be more than four experiments or activities that constitute a unit. When the experiment at one table is completed by all the science partners, the new experiment would be set up to take its place.

It is necessary to familiarize the child with the scientific terminology corresponding to the unit of study through the use of vocabulary charts. Each word on the chart is defined and illustrated in a booklet.

All the materials needed for the experiments are found at their respective tables. Also, the detailed, step-by-step instructions for the experiments are taped at each table for the children's use.

The children work in heterogeneous pairs within the group at each table in the Science Shop. Each set of partners is responsible for completing the experiments and writing the reports.

UNITS OF CONCENTRATION

Some of the units that can be studied in the Science Shop are:

Weather Magnetism
Light Plants
Rocks Electricity
Planets Animals
Heat

The instructions for the experiments or activities and the report forms for a unit are compiled in a packet for the children. The sample unit presented is on Electricity.* This unit consists of a vocabulary chart and four experiments.

Some of the words that could be found on a Vocabulary Chart about electricity are:

battery   circuit
conductors   insulators
electromagnet   dry cell
electrical energy   stored energy
energy of motion   chemical energy
motor   fuel

*A packet for this unit on Electricity would have these four experiments and a report form for each one. The circled numbers in each experiment are answered by the children on the report form; in addition, their findings are recorded.

TABLE 1: Light Bulb

Materials needed:

flashlight battery
miniature light bulbs
2 insulated wires, 10 inches long

Procedure:

1. Make the light bulb light up.
2. Set up an electrical circuit. Make a drawing of your circuit.
3. Answer these questions:

What kinds of energy does the bulb give off?
What part of the bulb gives off the light energy?
What happens when the wires touch the battery?
What happens when the wire or wires are not touching the battery?

TABLE 2: Electricity as Conductors and Insulators

Materials needed:

miniature light bulb

2 insulated wires
battery
pieces of plastic, aluminum, rubber, brass, paper, wood, metal

Procedure:

1. Set up the bulb and the battery so that the bulb lights up.
2. Disconnect one of the wires from the battery. Place the plastic strip so that one end touches the battery and the other end the wire, completing a circuit.
3. Does the lamp bulb light? Is this piece a conductor of electricity or an insulator?
4. Remove the piece of plastic and try the other pieces one at a time.
5. Which pieces are conductors and which are insulators?

TABLE 3: The Electric Bell

Materials needed:

1 electric bell
4 wires
2 D cells

Procedure:

1. Connect the bell, the wires, and the D cells so the bell will ring.
2. Draw a diagram of your electric bell circuit.
3. Look inside the bell. Make the bell ring again and watch what happens inside the bell.
4. What happens inside?
5. What do the electromagnets inside the bell do?

TABLE 4: Electromagnets

Materials needed:

washers
large nail
5 feet of insulated wire
D cell

Procedure:

1. Leaving one foot of wire, start wrapping the rest of the wire around the

nail, keeping it tight and close together. Cover most of the nail with the wire and then start back over the first layer.

2. Keep winding the wire back and forth on the nail until you have one foot of wire left.
3. Connect the ends of the wires to the battery.
4. Touch the nail of the electromagnet to the washers.
5. What happens?
6. How many washers can you pick up at one time? Record your results.

SCIENCE REPORT FORM
What you used:
What you did:
What happened:
How do you explain what happened?

During pre-workshop time we assign the science partners in one group a table to be completed during that workshop time. When the partners finish a table and have their reports checked, they proceed to a new experiment and table if vacant.

Let's look at a specific group and follow them through the four tables at the Science Shop. All the children are ready to study the unit on electricity. There are ten people in Nancy's group, five sets of partners. To begin with each set of partners is referred to one of the tables. Since the partners progress at different rates, some of them will finish the experiment during the allotted time and some will not. The assignment for subsequent periods may look something like Figure 4-1. If all tables are in operation or a set of partners has completed all the experiments, they would proceed to the Scientists' Lab where additional enrichment activities can be found.

SCIENTISTS' LAB

In the Scientists' Lab the partners choose a topic they would like to explore. The topic is pursued through the different activities found at the four stations. Each station has a folder for each topic. The child must do one of the listed activities in the topic folder.

Station one utilizes filmstrips, films, records, and tapes.

Station two presents a variety of report titles.

Station three is the construction of diagrams, charts, transparencies, slides, pictures, and table displays.

Station four is where the children do a mini-experiment for their topic.

A detailed explanation of the materials and the contents of the topic folders at each station follows.

Nancy's Group	10/25	11/2			
Nancy **Don**	finish T. 3	Vocab. Chart Start T. 4			
Art **Judy**	Start T. 4	Finish T. 4			
Ann **Dave**	Start T. 1	Finish T. 1			
Bill **Fred**	Start T. 2	Start T. 3			
Pat **Tim**	Do Vocab. Chart	Start T. 2			

ELECTRICITY

FIGURE 4-1: Science Shop Assignments

STATION ONE

The materials needed at this station are filmstrips, projector, large poster board or oaktag, and Magic Markers.

The science partners choose one filmstrip from a series dealing with one science concept. After viewing the filmstrip, the partners create a poster depicting the main idea.

STATION TWO

Necessary items found at this station are report title cards, paper, assortment of science books, tape recorder, cassette tapes. Cards with titles of famous scientists, scientific concepts, scientific discoveries and so forth, are kept at this station. Examples of some report titles and their topic titles are as follows:

DESERT ANIMALS

Desert Land
Roadrunner
Coyote
Ring-tailed Cat

Pack Rat
Gila Monster
Rattlesnake
Jack Rabbit

Prairie Dog
Deserts of the U.S.A.

SOLAR SYSTEM

Moon
Stars
What Is an Eclipse?
What Are Tides?
Sun
Mercury
Venus
Earth
Mars
Jupiter
Saturn
Uranus
Neptune
Pluto
Meteors
Comets
Revolution
Rotation

INSECTS

Moths
Grasshoppers
Wasps
Butterflies
Drone Bees
Queen Bee
Praying Mantis
Mosquito
Bumblebees
Ants
Worker Bee
Honeybees

WATER

Types of Irrigation
What Is Evaporation?
Water Cycle
Wells
Characteristics of Swamps
What Do Dams Do for Us?
Hoover Dam

Lakes
Dikes
Oasis
Quicksand
Oceans
Grand Coulee Dam
Levees

ROCKS

Igneous Rock
Sedimentary Rock
Metamorphic Rock
What Are Volcanoes?
Mountains
Minerals
How Are Diamonds Formed?
How Is Petrified Wood Made?
Recycling Process

ANIMAL GROUPS

Animals with One Cell
Worms
Jellyfishes
Sponges
Animals with Spiny Skins
Mammals
Birds
Reptiles
Amphibians
Fishes
Animals with Jointed Legs
Animals with Soft Bodies and Hard
  Shells
Invertebrates
Vertebrates

SEA ANIMALS

Octopus
Seals
Penguins
Sea Land
Shark
Dolphins
Whale
Salmon

Trout
Tuna
Walrus
Squid
Shrimp
Lobster
Clams
Snails
Goldfish—Angel Fish

JUNGLE ANIMALS

Jungle Land
Crocodile
Hippopotamus
Gorilla
Monkey
Leopard
Lion
Antelope
Giraffe
Elephant
Zebra

CLOTHING

Cloth from Mammals
Cloth from Insects
Cloth from Plants
Man-made Cloth
Weaving
Fibers
Story of Cotton
What Do Moths Do to Cloth?
Mildew

WEATHER

Types of Wind
Kinds of Precipitation
Clouds
Evaporation
Condensation
Weather Instruments
Seasons
Earth's Orbit
Earth's Axis
Climate Zones

AIR

Air Pollution
Atmospheres
How Do Birds Fly?
How Do Airplanes Fly?
Helicopters
Compressed Air
Air
Climate
Gases Found in the Air
Gravity
How Do Fish Breathe?

MACHINES

Levers
Wheels
Wedges
Pulleys
Inclined Planes
Conveyer Belts
Pumps
Elevators
Wheel and Axle
Block and Tackle
Screw
How a Printing Press Works

MOLECULES

Solid
Liquid
Gas
Molecules
How Do You Make Glass?
Distillation
Crude Oil
Expansion
Contraction
Matter
Physical Change
Chemical Change
Compounds
Elements
Atoms

PLANTS

Chlorophyll
Bulbs
How Are Bananas Grown?
How Do We Get Sugar?
How Is Pollen Carried?
What Is a Seed?
Different Ways Seeds Travel
Germination
Why Do We Need Plants?
Trees
Mushrooms
Mold—Yeast
Hybrid
Leaves
How Are the Parts of a Tree Useful?

SCIENTISTS

Archimedes

Johann Gutenberg
William Harvey
Galileo
Anton Van Leeuwenhoek
James Watt
Michael Faraday
Henry Bessemer
Edward Jenner
Robert Goddard
Luther Burbank
Jonas Salk
Louis Pasteur
Guglielmo Marconi
Walter Reed
George Washington Carver
Thomas Edison
William Herschel
Alexander Fleming

The science partners select a card and, using the available science books and reference materials, write a report. Along with the written report, children construct visual aids to be used in a table display from various media. After practice reciting the written report the children tape it. These science tapes and visual aids may then be used in the A. V. Shop.

STATION THREE

Essentials needed at this station are clear acetate sheets for transparencies, pieces of acetate (1½ "× 1½ ") for slides, cardboard for slides (2 "× 2 " of oaktag), colored projection pens, and glue.

At this station, the science partners prepare transparencies, slides, charts, diagrams, pictures, or displays to correspond with their lab topics. Some examples of activities to do at this station are:

Desert Animals

1. Draw what the desert would look like. Include the plants and animals of the desert.
2. Make a book of desert animals. Write one fact about each animal.
3. Make a picture chart of some desert animals and tell what each one eats. Label the animals.

Jungle Animals

1. Choose five animals to draw. Label them, including their habitat and their enemies.
2. Draw what the jungle would look like.
3. Draw the jungle animals on different colors of construction paper. Cut them out, mount them on large paper, and label them.

Solar System

1. Make a diagram showing the difference between revolution and rotation.
2. Make a diagram showing the Big Dipper, the Little Dipper.
3. Find out how many moons each planet has. Draw the planets with the correct number of moons around them.
4. Draw a picture of the moon, showing its mountains and valleys.
5. Make a moon chart of the drawings of the moon every day for a month.

Clothing

1. Draw an animal, an insect, and a plant, and tell the kind of cloth that came from each one.
2. Make a diagram showing the cycle of cotton.
3. Make a chart showing different weaving stitches and patterns. Label the stitches.

Weather

1. Make a picture diagram showing the different kinds of weather symbols.
2. Draw pictures of the different kinds of precipitation. Label them.
3. Make a chart of the different kinds of weather instruments.

Insects

1. Choose five insects to draw. Label the important parts (jointed legs, thorax, subthorax, wings, and antennae).
2. Make a diagram of the stages of the butterfly.
3. Draw one of the insects. Label it. Write three facts about the insect.
4. Make a diagram of the bee's home.

Air

1. Picture or chart of the types of air pollution.
2. Diagram of the different kinds of atmospheres. Label them.
3. Diagram and label a jet engine.

Water

1. Pictures of different kinds of irrigation. Label the types of irrigation.
2. Picture of an oasis.

3. Make a picture chart of the uses of water.
4. Diagram of the water cycle. Label its parts.

Machines

1. Diagram of how a lever works.
2. Pictures of types of wedges.
3. Chart with the different kinds of nails and how each is used.
4. Diagram of how an elevator works.
5. Diagram of how a pulley works.

Rocks

1. Chart showing the differences between rocks and minerals.
2. Trace the path of returnable and nonreturnable bottles in the recycling process.
3. Bulletin Board showing the steps in the production of steel *or* oil *or* aluminum.
4. Draw pictures of different rocks. Name each rock and tell if it is igneous, sedimentary, or metamorphic.
5. Collect rocks and put them in rock categories.

Molecules

1. Picture showing the solid, liquid, and gas substances on our planet.
2. Show examples between physical change and chemical change.
3. Diagram or chart or display showing the substances that are elements and the substances that are compounds.

Animal Groups

1. Draw pictures of the animals from *one* group. Label them. Write one fact about the group.
2. Make a chart showing the differences between warm-blooded and cold-blooded animals.
3. Label the parts of the inside of a worm.
4. Make a chart including one animal from each group, telling the food it eats, its habitat and its enemies.

Plants

1. Picture story or diagram showing how a tree becomes lumber.
2. Picture or chart showing the different ways seeds travel.
3. Diagram showing how wood is made into paper.
4. Diagram of a flower. Label its parts.
5. Collect leaves. Mount and label them.
6. Display of the different kinds of seeds. Label them.
7. Picture showing the foods that come from plants. Label the foods and plants.

Sea Animals

1. Make a chart of sea life which you eat. Include the animals, pictures, and one fact about each animal.
2. Make a large picture of undersea life.
3. Make a chart of sea life in the cold seas.
4. Make a chart of five sea animals listing the animal, the classification of the animal, the habitat, and the diet of the animal.

Scientists

1. Chart showing how milk is pasteurized.
2. Chart of Edison's inventions.
3. Diagram of the heart and the circulation of the blood throughout the body.
4. Chart of the Morse code of dots and dashes.
5. Diagram of a microscope. Label its parts.
6. Picture chart showing the products made from a peanut.

How to Make a Slide

The easiest way to prepare a slide is to use the cardboard rims from a commercial slide. To remove the old slide, separate the cardboard rims at the bottom.

If you do not have a commercial slide, cut 2″ by 2″ pieces of oaktag. Center a 1″ square in the middle of the 2″ square and cut it out carefully, using a razor blade or an X-acto knife. Insert your clear piece of acetate and glue the frame back together. Then draw.

The finished projects at this station may then be shown to a small group, the whole group, another class, or in the A.V. Shop.

STATION FOUR

Mini-experiments are housed at station four. All the materials for an experiment are at this station along with the question presenting the problem.

Here are a few ideas:

Any of the Animal Topics

1. Make clay models of the animals.

Solar System

1. Make clay ball models of the planets. Arrange them in order of smallest to largest. Label them.

Clothing

1. Place a wool sock and a cotton sock in water. What do you notice about the two?

Weather

1. Collect weather forecasts from the newspaper for a week. Check the temperature and the forecast for each day yourself and record your findings. How accurate was the newspaper's forecasts in relation to yours?

Water

1. Fill one bowl part way with water. Using the plastic tube, transfer the water from one bowl to the other.

Rocks

1. Test some rocks for sandiness. Rub two pieces of rock together. Do the grains of sand rub off?
2. Test some rocks for hardness. Scratch two rocks together. The one that makes a scratch mark is harder.
3. Record all your findings.

Molecules

1. Using gumdrops, marshmallows, or jelly beans, make a model of sugar. Sugar has 6 atoms of C, 6 atoms of O, and 12 atoms of H.

Plants

1. Grow a potato or a carrot. What happens?
2. Notice the difference between a plant that receives sunlight and one that is in a cupboard. Record what happens.

Scientists

1. Look at different things under the microscope. Draw what each item looks like and label them.

UNITS

To digress from the usual science table experiments we have some units designed with a variety of activities rather than only experiments. Units we have used are

> Dinosaurs
> Growing Plants
> Solar System
> Powders.

To give you a glimpse at how our science units are executed we will present our dinosaur unit.

A list of questions dealing with the dinosaur age is introduced to the children.

---

1. How do we know about dinosaurs?
2. What is a fossil?
3. What are dinosaurs like?
4. What does "dinosaur" mean?
5. How did dinosaurs get their names?
6. What is the Balance of Nature?
7. What kind of world did the dinosaurs live in?
8. Where were the dinosaurs found?
9. Why did the dinosaurs die out?

Step 1:

The science partners in the group choose a question to answer, making sure that no other partners have that question. They proceed to find their answer through the available dinosaur books from the library. After all the answers to the questions are found, the whole group discusses each question.

Step 2:

With the mood set, a list of dinosaurs is presented to the group. Dinosaurs included are: Allosaurus, Brontosaurus, Stegosaurus, Tyrannosaurus Rex, Diplodocus, Trachodon, Pteranodon, Ankylosaurus, Triceratops, Ornitholestes, and Brachiosaurus.

According to the number in the group each child should choose one, two, or three dinosaurs, until all dinosaurs are taken. They list all the facts that they can find about their dinosaur. This list is then transferred to a large chart, using Magic Markers.

Step 3:

On newsprint, the children practice drawing their chosen dinosaur in its environment. Once this is mastered, they draw on large white drawing paper, labeling their dinosaur.

Step 4:

The concluding activity is to create a diorama. With clay, make a model of the dinosaur studied. Paint a shoebox, inside and out. Each child should get his own materials for his diorama, including twigs, rocks, construction paper, colored cellophane paper, yarn, etc.

Using these materials, the children reconstruct the environment the dinosaur lived in.

5

The Reading Shop for Enjoyment and Enlightenment

READING —

—Getting involved in a world of adventure.
—Exploring the unknown.
—Going back into time.
—Wandering through the imaginary world.
—Delving into the future.
—Slipping into another's experiences.
—Satisfying the craving for knowledge.

The books that can be found in our Reading Shop are from individualized kits provided by the school and from personal libraries. These books are categorized into four levels, ranging from easy-to-read books to novels. For convenience we have them color-coded with colored tape. For example:

red—simple to read
blue—easy to read
yellow—short stories
green—novels

To keep order in the shop we have built homemade shelves from plywood and cement blocks. The wood and blocks are painted to coincide with the four levels (red books are found on red shelves, etc.).

A domain of books provides an atmosphere of enjoyment and fulfillment in the Reading Shop. To ignite this enthusiasm we use a number of motivational activities.

WEEKLY PREVIEWS

One activity creates interest by giving the students weekly previews of books from various levels. This is accomplished with the projection of an illustration on a transparency, along with a short introduction to the story. Be sure to end at a climactic point in the story, leaving the children in suspense. Later on in the year the children take the responsibility of preparing reviews of books they have read.

CLOWNING AROUND WITH BOOKS

Another activity revolves around the theme "Clowning Around with Books." Each child has his own clown with five balloons posted on a bulletin board. For every two books the child reads and reports on satisfactorily, he receives one of his balloons. (See Figure 5-1.)

FIGURE 5-1: Clowning Around with Books

BOOK-READING RACES

To spark a note of competition we occasionally have book-reading races between the boys and the girls. The duration of the race is two to three weeks. A chart can be used to keep track of the race. To get a mark on the chart the book must be read and the activity assigned completed. (Some examples of reading charts are shown in Figure 5-2.) At the end of the allotted time, the winners of the race are given a party with the treats provided by the losing team.

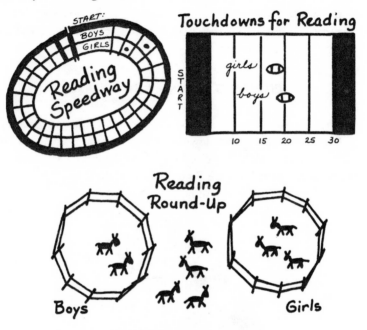

FIGURE 5-2: Book Reading Races

NAME PUZZLES

On 3″-wide strips of oaktag write each child's name with Magic Marker (Figure 5-3). Cut the name into six jigsaw-shaped pieces, numbering them on the back. Put each child's name puzzle in an envelope. When a book and its activities have been approved, the child posts the first puzzle piece on the bulletin board. The rest of the pieces are put up in sequence as books are read.

COLOR A PICTURE

Various objects can be used for keeping track of the number of books a child reads. One object is a butterfly. Each child is given his own butterfly which is cut from oaktag. The butterfly looks like Figure 5-4. Each time a

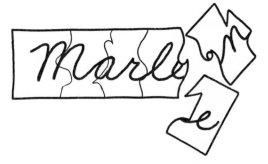

FIGURE 5-3: Name Puzzles

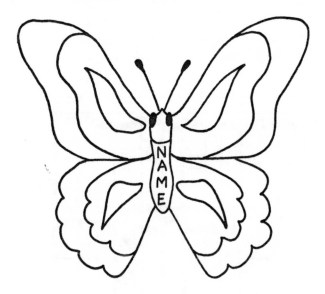

FIGURE 5-4: Reading Butterfly

book is read, the child colors in a section of his butterfly. Other objects which can be used in the same way are:

clowns	roosters
daisies	children in patchwork clothes
giraffes	turtles
umbrellas	

CLASS ADD-ONS

Through a group effort, the children try to reach the goal of completing the Reading Shop bulletin board. The idea of the bulletin board is to add on to it each time they complete a book. The theme could be one of the following:

> Volume Shelf
> Decorate a Christmas Tree
> An Animal Forest
> Title Collage

Volume Shelf

The number of bookshelves and the size of your volumes will depend upon the class size, the number of books you want the class to read, and the duration of the bulletin board project. When a child finishes a book, he fills out a title card which is then attached to a black book on the shelf. (See Figure 5-5.)

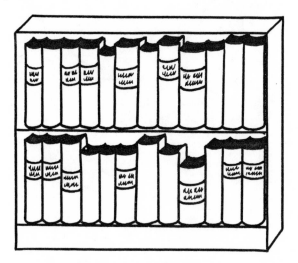

FIGURE 5-5: Volume Shelf

Decorate a Christmas Tree

Around the Holidays, trim your construction paper Christmas tree with ornaments of book titles. Decorate the ornaments with glitter, paints, sequins, etc.

To make a three-dimensional Christmas tree to hang these ornaments on you will need:

yarn
a large number of 6″×4½″ pieces of green construction paper

With the yarn, outline your Christmas tree on the bulletin board. Have the children fold the green pieces in half to 4½ "× 3 ". Cut slits and glue ends as shown in Figure 5-6. Then squash this like an accordion and staple a few appendages to the board. To make a life-like bushy tree staple the green pieces very close together—practically on top of each other. Then hang the title ornaments on the "branches" of your tree.

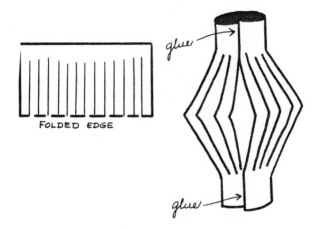

FIGURE 5-6: Christmas Tree Branches

An Animal Forest

Since children are invariably fond of animals, they enjoy making their own and contributing them to a class bulletin board. The animals they make can be real or make-believe, and the titles may be written on them. The children are eager to increase the number of forest animals.

Title Collage

To allow the children to design their own bulletin board, a title collage is created. Here the child writes his title and name on a colored piece of construction paper, cuts it out in the shape he wishes, and places it wherever he wants on the board.

BASIC READING PROGRAM

The basic reading program in the Reading Shop is a combination of written and oral reports. Through the use of these two avenues of reporting, both children who excel in speaking abilities and those who excel in writing abilities are given the chance to express themselves effectively.

Once a child has read his chosen book, he must do a written book report from one of the following six forms.

FORM 1

Name _____

Title of book _____

Author _____ Level _____

1. What character didn't you like in the story? _____

   _____

   Why? _____

2. List the most important events in order. _____

   _____

   _____

   _____

3. Did you like reading this book? _____

   Why? _____

   _____

4. The picture I liked best: page _____

5. On a sheet of drawing paper draw a picture that could be used as a cover for this book.

FORM 2

Name _____

Title of book _____

Author _____ Level _____

1. Tell something that you learned from this story.

   _____

   _____

2. Is this a real or a make-believe story? _____

   _____

3. Has anything like this ever happened to you?

   _____ If yes, then tell about it. _____

   _____

   _____

   _____

4. What happened at the end of the story? _____

   _____

   _____

5. On a sheet of drawing paper, draw a picture of your favorite character in the story.

FORM 3

Name _____

Title of book _____

Author _____ Level _____

1. Did you like this story? _____

   Why? _____

   _____

   _____

2. Describe one of the characters in the story. _____

   _____

   _____

   _____

3. Do you think your classmates would like to read this book? _____

   Why? _____

   _____

   _____

4. Think of a new title for this story. What would you call it? _____

5. Draw a picture that could be used as a cover for this book.

FORM 4

Name _____

Title of book _____

Author _____ Level _____

1. Name the important character in your story. _____

2. The part of the story I liked best is: _____

   _____

   _____

   _____

3. List of new words I learned in this story. _____

   _____

   _____

   _____

4. If you could choose a character to be your friend, who would you choose and why? _____

   _____

5. Draw a picture that shows your favorite part in the story.

FORM 5

Name _____

Title of book _____

Author _____ Level _____

1. Why did you choose this book? _____
   _____
   _____

2. Who is your favorite character? _____
   _____ Why? _____
   _____
   _____

3. What is the main problem in the story? _____
   _____
   _____
   _____

4. The picture I like best: Page _____
   Why? _____
   _____

5. Draw a picture about the story.

FORM 6

Name _____

Title of book _____

Author _____ Level _____

1. Use one word to describe the story. _____
   _____

2. What is the story about? _____
   _____
   _____
   _____

3. Name some of the characters in the story. _____
   _____
   _____

4. Which character did you like best? _____
   _____Why? _____
   _____
   _____

5. Draw a picture of an important event that took place in your story.

After completion of the written report the child has a conference with the teacher. At this time the written report is checked, questions are asked, and a portion of the book is read aloud. A great timesaving device we have discovered is the tape recorder. The child would tape his report according to the following posted procedure:

Answer these questions:

1. What is your name?
2. What is the title of your book?
3. Who is your favorite character? Why?
4. What part of the story did you like best? Why? What happened?
5. Would you like your classmates to read this book? Why?
6. What would your picture look like if you had to draw the front cover of the book?
7. Read a page.

An alternate form that could be used for oral reports is as follows:

Choose One:

1. Describe the book in one word.
2. Would you like your classmates to read this book? Why?
3. Why did you choose this book?
4. Which character didn't you like? Why?

Choose Two:

1. Say a word you did not know. Explain what it means.
2. Describe an event from the story.
3. Compare a character in the book to yourself. Who are you most like? How are you like him?

Choose One:

1. List the most important events in order.
2. What is the main problem in your story? How is it solved?

Oral Reading

ENRICHMENT ACTIVITIES

A change of pace is necessary to keep the children's interest alive. The following activities will give you a variety of projects to use in place of the reports. These activities may be grouped together to be used in place of the written and oral reports or they may be used separately as a second activity to either the written or oral reports.

Floating Bookcovers

Many teachers neglect a very serviceable part of the room—the ceiling. Circular bookcovers in various sizes can adorn your ceiling, making it a storybook wonderland. Using colored construction paper of different sizes, depict an event from a book, being sure to include the title. After the picture has been colored, staple it into a cylinder shape. Punch three holes in the top of the cylinder and hang with yarn.

Hanging Characters

This activity lends itself to emphasizing the importance of characters in a story. The child chooses the most important character in the story or his favorite character for this project. Starting with a construction paper body, he portrays the character, using materials such as yarn, material, construction paper, Magic Markers, crayons, paints, etc. Since the character is suspended from the ceiling, both the front and back sides must be depicted.

Vocabulary Booklet

To build a child's vocabulary, a booklet is made for each child to use. These are easy to make. Simply use 9″×6″construction paper covers with lined paper inside. For aesthetic looking covers, use an entertaining illustration such as the one shown in Figure 5-7. The booklet can be used for either one story or many. The number of pages inside will vary accordingly. While

FIGURE 5-7: Vocabulary Booklet Cover

the child is reading a book, he records any unfamiliar words from the story and the page numbers on which these words occur. Using the dictionary, he writes down the definitions of the words, and then uses each word in a sentence.

Cartoons

To stress the significance of the sequence of events, the children can make cartoon strips about their stories. After the four major steps in the story have been established, the child transforms them onto 9"X24" strips of drawing paper. The strips are divided into four equal frames, one for each event. The first frame includes the title of the book and the child's name. All the frames contain "balloons" representing a portion of the dialogue from the story.

Pick-a-Pal Paragraph

Character sketching and analysis are the themes of this project. The child first chooses from his story a character that he would like to have as his friend. On a 9"X12" piece of construction paper folded in half, the child draws this character involved in an event from the story. Inside the folder the child writes a paragraph telling why he chose the character, how they are alike or different, and what they would do if they were friends.

Diorama

A popular creation for children to make is the shoebox diorama. In this project a child displays an event from his story. Any materials that are available can be used as long as they help to achieve the desired effect.

Riddle Posters

Extra! Extra! Read all about it! This is the main idea behind the riddle posters. Each child is responsible for making a poster to promote the book he has read. Along with the illustrations about the book the child incorporates a "Who or what am I?" riddle. Since this is a promotional endeavor, the answer is not included. The children must read the book to find out the answer to the riddle. The materials that can be used for this project are 18"X24" oaktag or heavy white drawing paper and paints. (See Figure 5-8.)

FIGURE 5-8: Reading Riddle Poster

Creative Dramatics in Reading

Creative Dramatics can be utilized quite successfully in reading enrichment activities. Some suggested activities are as follows:

1. The child reads into the tape recorder his story or a representative chapter from a longer story, putting in sound effects whenever possible. The success of the oral reading depends upon the child's dramatic interpretation. This is another item that could be used to advantage in the A.V. Shop.
2. The child assumes the role of a movie producer as he writes his story in the form of a play. His job consists of casting the characters and directing the play to its final production.
3. Flannel board characters and scenery are the focal points of this storytelling project. The child retells the story in his own words, using the felt characters and scenery he has made as visual aids.
4. For a creative experience, the children develop a new adventure for the characters from the books they have read. The adventures are presented in the form of puppet plays, with the children making their character puppets.

6

Stimulating the Mind Through the Creative Writing Shop

Developing creativity in the child is especially important in all grade levels. No child is too young to start using his mind to a greater extent. Given free reign and a chance to work independently, a child's imagination can open up a whole new world for him.

The Creative Writing Shop gives each child a variety of activities which will motivate him and give him an opportunity for self-expression. We will show you the ideas we have tried and found successful. This chapter includes the following categories: charts, equipment, creative materials, supplies, record keeping, and sample units. Remember, it is not necessary to have a center for Creative Writing. The creative materials can be anywhere in the room, just so they are visible to the children and readily accessible.

CHARTS

To set the stage for creative writing, an environment of colorful, eye-catching charts is a helpful aid. In our area we have a specific section for creative writing. In the shop we have a large table and chairs, the charts, and all the creative writing materials close at hand for the children's use.

We have one chart (Figure 6-1) that illustrates the five important parts to include in a story. As can be seen by the illustration, the five points are depicted through the use of "Mr. Who," "Mr. What," "Mr. When," "Mr. Where," and "Mr. Why."

To familiarize the child with creative writing terms we have prepared a vocabulary chart with definitions. Some of the words included on the chart are:

Adventure	Illustrate
Appearance	Imagine
Autobiography	Incident
Biography	Make-believe
Character	Mystery
Description	Non-fiction
Experience	Nonsense
Fiction	Plot

FIGURE 6-1: Important Parts of a Story

Since one of our creative activities, the Idea Bin, is color-coded we have a chart (Figure 6-2) that explains which color stands for which activity. The Idea Bin is composed of many cards of different colors. For example, pink cards suggest titles for stories.

FIGURE 6-2: Idea Bin Chart

Many children enjoy writing their own poems. We have a chart (Figure 6-3) offering guidelines of different varieties of poems. The child may choose at a glance the style of poetry he wants to write.

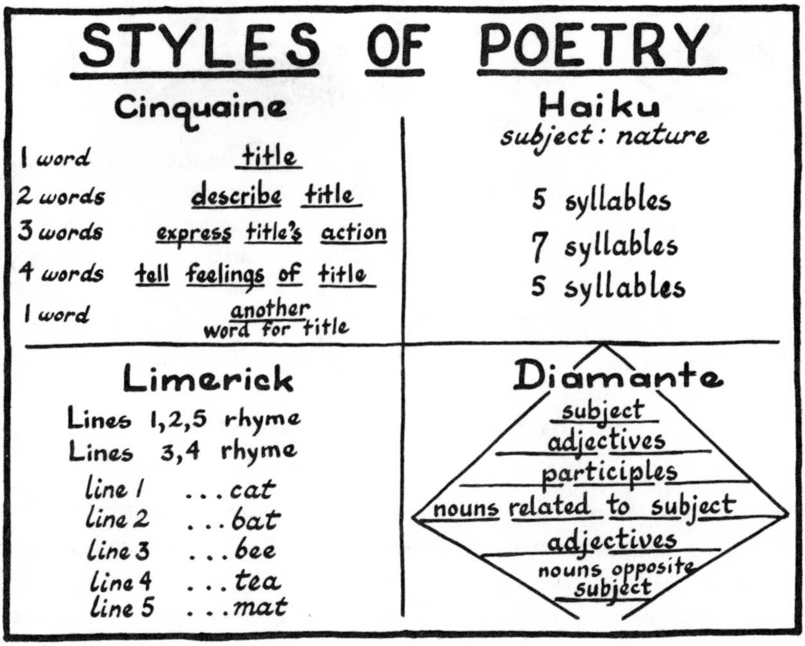

STYLES OF POETRY

Cinquaine

1 word	title
2 words	describe title
3 words	express title's action
4 words	tell feelings of title
1 word	another word for title

Haiku
subject: nature

5 syllables

7 syllables

5 syllables

Limerick

Lines 1,2,5 rhyme

Lines 3,4 rhyme

line 1 ...cat
line 2 ...bat
line 3 ...bee
line 4 ...tea
line 5 ...mat

Diamante

subject
adjectives
participles
nouns related to subject
adjectives
nouns opposite subject

FIGURE 6-3: Poetry Chart

EQUIPMENT

An additional feature in the Creative Writing Shop is the supplementary equipment. Elaborate equipment, however, is not a necessity for a workable Creative Writing Shop. In this section we will discuss the equipment we have and how we use it.

Perhaps the most useful piece of equipment is the light box (Figure 6-4), used for showing transparencies to a small group. This is particularly nice because it can be made very simply with materials close at hand. To construct the light box you will need only three materials: a large box, a piece of tissue paper, and a small high intensity lamp.

There are three other pieces of equipment that we have in the Creative Writing Shop. A typewriter is very exciting to children. It is not very often they get to use one. The uses of this piece of equipment are unlimited.

A tape recorder can be used to capture a child's inner thoughts before transcribing them on paper. Also, children love to make up stories and listen

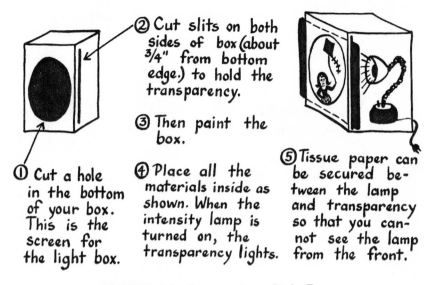

② Cut slits on both sides of box (about ¾" from bottom edge.) to hold the transparency.

③ Then paint the box.

① Cut a hole in the bottom of your box. This is the screen for the light box.

④ Place all the materials inside as shown. When the intensity lamp is turned on, the transparency lights.

⑤ Tissue paper can be secured between the lamp and transparency so that you cannot see the lamp from the front.

FIGURE 6-4: Constructing a Light Box

to their own voices on tape. Another activity is a continuous story made by the children. One at a time, the children tape a short event about a designated topic. After each child has recorded his part, the story is completed. For example, one topic could be "A Day in the Life of Robbie the Robot." The children's anticipation builds as they wait to listen to everybody's adventures put together.

The last valuable piece of equipment is the record player. One of the activities that children enjoy using it for is to complete a story that a record starts. Pick up the needle at a climactic point and then let the children carry on. Another activity involving the use of the record player is for the children to create their own poem or story inspired by the mood music they listen to.

CREATIVE MATERIAL

Tantalizing . . .

diversified . . .

spicy . . .

These words describe the materials we use in the Creative Writing Shop. To keep the child's interest we have readily available a multitude of provocative ideas and activities. This prevents the children from falling into the humdrum routine of one activity.

1. CARD FILE

The card file consists of 4½ "× 6" colored cards. There are four different colors of cards:

A. Green Cards—Report Titles

Research this title, and make a booklet about it. Include everything that is important about it. Pictures too!

Some of the report titles on the green cards are:

A Constellation	Ants
Comets	Baseball
Braille	Astronomy
Unicycles	Clouds
Sponges	Witches
Boomerangs	Airports
Bowling	What Is Lava?
Cheese	Magic
Rockets	Alphabet
Scientists	Dolphins
Castles	Canals
Harry Houdini	What Is a Tsetse Fly?
A Jungle Animal	The Sphinx
All About Trains	Deserts
Zebras	Archery
Submarines	X-rays
Rocks	Butterflies
Your Skin and Its Sense of Touch	Your Sense of Hearing
Cards with Famous Flowers	What Is Hieroglyphics?
Cards with Political Figures	Cards with Authors
Cards with Inventors	Cards with States
Cards with Sports Figures	Cards with Presidents

Cards with Monuments, Memorials, Statues

B. Orange Cards—Story Starters

These sentences must be the first sentence in your story.

— I was walking along the beach when suddenly . . .
— The children were playing on the beach when they found the strange footprints, and they decided to follow them . . .
— I dialed a number and guess who answered . . .
— Once upon a time, long, long ago . . .

— If I could be an object, I would be a . . .

— I can hardly wait until . . .

— If I were a giant . . .

— If I were the last person left on earth . . .

— George Washington would be surprised if . . .

— This is a good day for me today . . .

— If I were in Never-Never Land, I would . . .

— If my ruler were only a magic wand I . . .

— If I were as small as Tom Thumb . . .

— The day I went to the moon, I . . .

— I get very angry when . . .

— If I had a million dollars . . .

— My dad is funny when . . .

— It was not quite ten o'clock when . . .

— Early one July morning I woke up to find Sherlock Holmes standing by my bed . . .

— If I had a magic pair of boots I would . . .

— I was really scared when . . .

— Mary knew that if her mother found out, she wouldn't be able to sit down for days, but she was determined to carry out her plan . . .

— I opened the door suddenly and . . .

— At first, the noise was very faint and seemed far away. It was an odd noise, one that the boys didn't recognize. As it moved closer, they went out to see what it might be . . .

— Bill walked to the window to let in a little air. As he began to raise it, something outside caught his eye. He stood there with his mouth open . . .

— Andy moved to a new neighborhood and when he tried to make friends . . .

— It was on a chilly evening that I met the boy named . . .

— I wish somebody would invent . . .

— If I were invisible . . .

— I am the brakes on your car . . .

— I love school when . . .

C. Pink Cards—*Titles* for Your Story

Read this title, then think of a good story to go with it, and write it.

How the Lion Got His Roar	My Ambition
Why the Owl Says "Who"	The Dragon in the Box
If I Were the Mayor	Muscles the Monkey
The Day I Met the President	Beanie the Baby Bunny
It Happened at the Magic Show	A Trip on a Raft
The Day All the Lights Went Off	The Most Fun I Ever Had

The Great Automobile Race	The Mysterious Box
A Bear in the Camp	My Little Invisible Pet
Danger!	The Lonely Stegosaurus
The Day I Was Invisible	The Adventure of a Penny
Silly Willie the Baby Elephant	A Trick for April Fool's Day
The Night of the Big Blizzard	The Haunted Castle
The Runaway Engine	The Camper

You Should Have Been with Me the Day I Met the Witch

Being Twelve Feet Tall Gives a Person a Lot of Problems

D. Yellow Cards—*Ideas* to Write About

Read the suggestion on the card and write your own story.

— Write an amusing story about a food with an interesting name. (Or, How did it get its name?)

> upside-down cake
> apple turnovers
> angel-food cake
> devil's-food cake
> or make up your own.

— Write a story about what you think your pencil and paper talked about last night.

— *What if* a plane landed on the school playground one day?

— Describe what a secret is.

— Describe to a man from outer space what school is.

— Choose a product that you can buy in a store. Then write a commercial for it, trying to sell your product.

— If someone gave you three wishes, what would you wish for?

— What are some of the sounds you would hear if you were standing on a street corner? Tell of your adventures.

— Describe how high is up?

— *What if* you saw a zebra grazing in front of your house one morning?

— You found an old wallet with $50 in it. What were your experiences in trying to locate the owner?

— Imagine: You are to interview a famous person. What happened?

— Who would you most like to be if you could be anyone in the world?

— *What if* you found a turtle in your bathtub?

— Draw a picture of something you have never seen before. Then write and tell us what you will call it, and what it does.

— What is your favorite color? Explain why.

— *What if* you were traveling across the mountains in a covered wagon a hundred years ago?

—Write a mystery story about these three words: ghost; hill; storm.

—Write a space adventure. Imagine that you built your own rocket and went to the moon. What happened to you up there? What did you see?

—Tell what age you would like to be. Why?

—*What if* all the lights in your house went off every time you turned on the water?

—What would you do if you came to school late, and found *nobody* in the room.

—Tell about where you would fly if you had wings.

—Write an autobiography.

—*Answer this question:* What are tears for?

—What would a cookie jar and a refrigerator say to each other in a house with ten children in it?

—If you met an animal that could talk, what would you talk to him about?

—A pirate captures you and hides you on his boat. Tell of your adventures on the boat until you are rescued.

—What if you are a stowaway on a ship?

—Write a story—a funny story—using these three things in it: map; dog; carpet.

—What is the funniest thing you ever saw?

—What would you do if you suddenly discovered that you were only one inch tall?

—Invent your own machine. Draw us a picture of your machine. Then write and tell how it works.

2. PICTURE FILE

The most popular activity is the picture file. This consists of various pictures from magazines mounted on construction paper. Children have a vivid imagination; when shown a picture they see many different things. The stories from one picture are as many and as varied as the children themselves.

3. HEADLINE FILE

Newspaper headlines are a source of creative writing material. Any catchy headline that you may come across may be used in this file. These, like the pictures, are mounted on construction paper.

4. TRANSPARENCIES

You may use either commercially prepared transparencies or prepare your own transparencies. Picture transparencies can service a small group using the light box or a large group using the overhead.

An easy way to prepare your own transparencies is to use the *color lift* method, by the aid of a Dry Mount Press. This method involves seven steps:

1st step: Make sure that the picture you want to use is printed on a clay coated paper stock. To check this, simply wet your finger and rub it back and forth on the surface and if a milky, white coat comes off on your finger, then you have a clay coated picture.

2nd step: You can make two transparencies at once and save yourself some time. Place two pictures of the same size back to back, with the pictures you want to reproduce facing out, or you can make two transparencies from a single page printed on both sides.

3rd step: Place these pictures between two pieces of laminating film about 12 "× 9" (these will be trimmed later). These are then sandwiched between a clean piece of paper and placed in the preheated press for about 1½-2 minutes at 275 degrees.

4th step: When you have the materials out of the press, you may want to trim the pictures to fit a certain size frame (if you plan to use a frame). If two pages have been laminated back to back, they will separate easily as soon as you cut into the paper on one side.

5th step: Submerge this film into warm sudsy water (using a mild detergent) and let soak for about 5-10 minutes. If adequately soaked, the paper will peel off in a single sheet. The printed image will remain on the film —transferred by heat and pressure.

6th step: After removing the paper, wet the film again. Then, using a sponge or soft cloth, gently wipe off the white clay coating that remains on the film. Rinse, and hang or lay flat to dry. Blot film with paper towels if you want to speed drying.

7th step: When the transparency is dry, you may laminate it a second time, both to protect the printed image and to add "body" for easy filing or handling. These may now be carefully trimmed and securely mounted on a cardboard frame by taping all four edges to the underside of the frame.

And you are now ready to use your own homemade transparencies.

5. PICK-A-STORY

Three large cans make up our Pick-a-Story activity. One can contains cards suggesting characters for a story (*who*); another can contains situation cards (*what*); and the last can contains cards with names of places (*where*). The child creates his own story by choosing one to three character cards, one *what* card, and one *where* card.

Who	*What*	*Where*
tired boy	a race	on the lake
lazy girl	a field trip	at school
happy mother	a vacation	on the mountain
excited father	an earthquake	in the jungle
lonely dinosaur	a waterfall	on a boat
sleepy bird	a tornado	in the sky
butterfly	a swamp	at the hospital
nasty fish	an explosion	at the beach
flower	a dinner	on television
teacher	a canyon	on stage
angry dog	a birthday	in a rocket
sick cat	a stomach ache	in the aquarium
missing monkey	a conversation	in the car
baby bunny	a song	in a tree
singing seal	a foreign language	at the university
astronaut	a competitive game	in the forest
camper	a play	in the park
doctor	a television show	in the desert
salesman	an animal trap	in a store
singer	a party	at home
skier	a book	in a tent
sailor	a movie	at the zoo
swimmer	a pain	on the farm
sister	a painting	at the theater
brother	a campfire	in the backyard
grandma	a forest fire	on the moon
grandpa	a litterbug	at the circus
actor	a musical harmonica	on a bus
actress	an expedition	on a bicycle
student	a midnight cruise	downtown

6. COMPOSER'S KIT

The Composer's Kit (Figure 6-5) is similar to the picture file discussed earlier. The only difference is that the child gets a manila folder which has the vocabulary words he must use, the picture, and the title of the story.

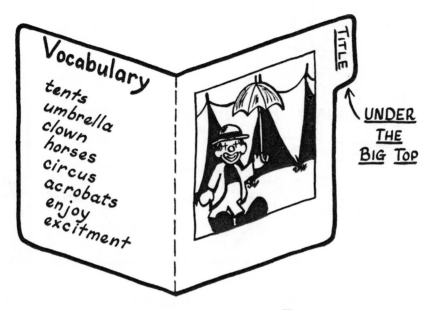

FIGURE 6-5: Composer's Kit

7. EVERYDAY DICTIONARIES

Some children may want to know how to spell a very commonly used word, but may not want to take the time to look it up. It is for this reason that the class makes up its own Everyday Dictionary (Figure 6-6). This is kept in a handy place so that any child may use it at any time. Each page has just one word on it with a sentence using that word. If a child comes across a word he cannot spell and it is not already in the dictionary, he goes to the teacher who will then enter his word and sentence in the book. This way, the book continues to grow and grow.

This is a very successful activity, and the children enjoy using their dictionaries. They are very easily constructed, using heavy paper for covers and dividers, and regular paper for the pages. It is advisable to use paper fasteners to keep the book together, so that extra pages may be added. We have also found it advantageous to break the alphabet down into about three or four books so that more than one person may use them at the same time. The children will certainly enjoy trying to think of words as well as the sentences for *their* dictionary.

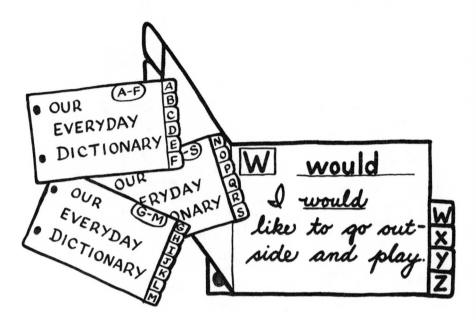

FIGURE 6-6: Everyday Dictionaries

8.   OBJECTS

For a change of pace from the card files, you can shift the children's creative interest to objects. Some examples are:

old torn-up shoe	dirty baby bottle
set of keys	piece of candy
lantern	old-fashioned candle holder
old well-worn hat	old book
fishing rod	broken vase
old doll	slingshot
cracked mirror	present
balloon	pocket watch
old wallet	picnic basket
cane	ring
skeleton key	feathered ink pen
pair of old glasses	empty pop bottle

can opener	toothbrush
paint brush with paint	old tire
cookie jar	ladder
hammer	crumpled piece of paper
chewed-up pencil	old stool
jack	toothpaste roller-upper
funny kitchen gadgets	unusual tools

Three different activities can be used with these objects. The first activity, helpful in directing beginning writers, is to ask specific questions about the object. In their stories they must include the answers to the questions. The second activity, used later in the year, does not guide the children through the use of questions. In this activity, you set the object on the table and let the children write what they want. The third activity is to bring in tools and gadgets that the children have not seen before. Let them make up directions for their use.

9. SUPPLIES

Some of the essential supplies that should be available to the children in the Creative Writing Shop are:

dictionaries	stapler	crayons
pencils	colored pencils	hole punch
construction paper	paper	yarn
paste	rulers	Magic Markers
scissors	drawing paper	

10. UNITS

A. Write a Book

This is a unit we have used in our Creative Writing Shop with great success. The children are given three alternatives: to write an adventure story; to write a book of poems; or to write a biography of an adult they know. Let's take a look at each one of these choices.

The adventure story must consist of at least three chapters. The child decides the characters he wants in his story, the plot, and the title. Then he must have a main idea for each chapter. After the work completed thus far is discussed with the teacher, the child proceeds to write the first chapter. The final product is put into book form, complete with cover, title page, and illustrations for each page.

The book of poems, the second choice, must have limitations as to topics. The child selects three or four general areas that he would like to write poems about. Examples of topics are flowers, magic, birds, people, cities, and sports. The child writes at least three poems about each topic. The poems may be in free form or conventional styles such as haiku, cinquaines, limericks, etc. These poems are put into book form with illustrations and a table of contents.

The third book is a biography about an adult. In this book the emphasis should be on interesting aspects of the person's life rather than on solely factual information. Needless to say, outside work is necessary for this project. The child must interview the person and learn as much as he can about the person's life. Illustrations also accompany this finished book.

B. Playwriting

The development of a well-rounded child requires working cooperatively with his peers as well as working independently. The Write-a-Book Unit involves individual effort while the Playwriting Unit is a group effort. Divide the children into groups of approximately seven children. Each group must have a leader and a recorder. During Workshop Time, the Creative Writing group will begin by discussing ideas and plots for their play. Once that has been accomplished, the next step is to pick the characters they want in the play. Next, an outline of all the things that will happen in the play should be written. From this point, the group begins writing the dialogue in the play. After the play has been written and cast, the children work on the scenery and rehearse. The final project is a result of the children's writing, producing, directing, scenery-making, and acting.

A variation of this unit can be illustrated by a girl, Tandra, who wrote an entire play, *The Haunted Castle*. She chose the cast, and directed the production to its completion. Tandra and her cast worked on the play when their assigned work was finished and during recess. After devoting three weeks to this project, they presented it to the entire class. They received a standing ovation for a job well done.

C. Class Book

To maintain enthusiasm, each week we choose the best story written to be put into a class book. The selected story is re-written on good paper, correcting grammatical errors and misspellings. An illustration for the story is also made. The children are eager to see how many stories they can contribute to the class book. The book is constantly on display in our area to the children and visitors.

The creative writing ideas we have presented to you will hopefully give you a start in preparing your own shop. Don't think you have to use all of this material. Add to it, revise it, flavor it with your own style. We have enjoyed reading the children's stories and learning more about our pupils through their work.

7

Developing Vocabulary in the Spelling Shop

There are two kinds of communication—oral and written. For effective written communication, good spelling is essential. Spelling includes utilization of reading and phonics skills. Along with these are needed repetition and memorization of the spelling words. This can be accomplished by games and continuous studying of the words. Some forms of practicing the words are typing, using transparencies, writing on the chalkboard, writing in sand or salt, using alphabet macaroni, and newspaper letters.

The games we have available in the Spelling Shop are:

Raindrop Game

Defo

Match Game

Password

Tic Tac Toe

Spell It

Battle Stations

Drag Race

Concentration

Spelling Darts

Paper Games

How Many

Dictionary Search

Initial Dot

Spelling Designs

Raindrop Game

Materials needed:

6 pieces of heavy cardboard, 10″× 12″
wooden cube
4 different colors of construction paper
1 cardboard piece, 10″× 10″

On each color of construction paper, trace 20 raindrops approximately the size of a half-dollar. Write words on the raindrops that you want your children to know how to spell. If desired, each color can stand for words all dealing with a specific spelling pattern. Laminate the raindrops and cut them out.

On each of the six cardboards there is an umbrella which is divided into 12 sections, each large enough to place a raindrop on. (See Figure 7-1.) The 10″ × 10″ cardboard is used for the placement of the raindrops during the game (Figure 7-2).

Four sides of the cube are painted according to the colors of the raindrops and on the other two sides are written "Skip a turn" and "Any color."

FIGURE 7-1: Raindrop Game

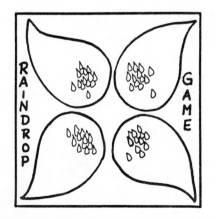

FIGURE 7-2: Raindrop Game Center Board

To play:

The object of the game is to fill the umbrella with raindrops. The first player rolls the cube and draws the raindrops as designated by the cube. He reads the word on the raindrop. The player on his right is to spell the word correctly in order to win the raindrop for his umbrella. If he cannot spell it, the player who reads it gets to place it on his card. This continues until a player has successfully filled his card.

Defo

Materials needed:

lists of spelling words
oaktag, 10"× 10"
construction paper, 2"× 3"
small pieces of construction paper, macaroni, discs, etc. (anything suitable as markers)

Defo is a type of bingo game. Its objective is to reinforce the spelling and definitions of words. Make up lists of 30 words that you want your children to be familiar with. On the 2"×3" cards, write the definitions of the words on the lists. Each list and its definition cards should be the same color to avoid confusion.

On the oaktag draw an empty bingo chart with five blocks across and five blocks down, the middle block being a "free" space. Laminate these so they can be used repeatedly.

To play:

Each player fills the space on his bingo chart with words from the vocabulary list. He uses a grease pencil for this. Using the corresponding definition cards, the caller reads the meanings to the players. The players try to find on their card the word that fits the definition. When they find the word, they cover it. The first player with five in a row wins.

Match Game

Materials needed:

construction paper cards, 6"× 3"
transparencies
grease or projection pencils

To play:

Divide the group into equal teams with one person as a caller. The object of the game is for the team members to match the answers to questions the caller asks. It is not a match unless all words are spelled correctly. The team members write their answers on a transparency with a grease pencil.

Some of the questions that could be used on the 6"× 3" cards are:

Name a room in a house.
Name a kitchen appliance.
Will you_____with me?
We sell _____at our store.
Name something you have in your desk.
Name an article of clothing.
Name an animal.
Name something that is round.
Where are my_____?
Name something that is cold.
Name a musical instrument.
I broke my_____.
Don't fall on the _____.
Name a holiday.
Name a fruit.
Name a kind of meat.
Name a color.
Name a sport.
Name something kept in the refrigerator.
Name a flower.
Name a flavor of ice cream.
Name a month.
Name a season of the year.
I want to plant _____ in my garden.
Who broke my _____?
I can't _____ it.
Name a piece of furniture.
Name something that is in the sky.
My dog's name is_____.
Name something that is smooth.
Name a school subject.
My_____has gone home.
Name something you would buy in a dime store.
Name something to drink.
On a Saturday morning I like to_____.

To score:

Five points are given for every match. The team that is ahead at the end of a given time or the first to reach a set score wins.

Password

Materials needed:

construction paper cards, 3"×3"

To play:

The words that are used on the cards can be the child's spelling words or words that he is familiar with. Make two sets. There are two teams, consisting of two players each, a caller, and a scorekeeper. The object of the game is for one teammate to guess the word on the card from his teammate's one-word clue. The caller must be sure to give the same word to each team.

To score:

One point is scored for guessing the word. A second point is added if the teammate spells the word correctly.

Some words that can be written on the cards are:

home	flower	cloud
rainbow	worm	lizard
book	piano	hate
bell	picture	love
sad	state	swim
listen	country	dance
happy	automobile	gallop
lawn	television	puppet
lawyer	theater	movie
mansion	sound	medicine
radio	whisper	island
tunnel	polish	cricket
postcard	orange	open
operation	crazy	metal
gold	contest	kite
wood	guilty	innocent
rocket	heart	heavy
pillow	prompt	glove
birthday	blind	mattress

Tic Tac Toe

Tic Tac Toe can be played through two different media. To play the game on the floor you need four long strands of yarn and five X and O cards. Arrange the yarn to make a tic-tac-toe pattern. Since only three people use the equipment for one game, several sets can be made to involve a larger number of children. Using his spelling book, the caller asks a child to spell a word. If he spells it correctly he gets to place his X or O card in a strategic place on the board. The player that gets three cards in a row first wins and switches places with the caller.

Tic Tac Toe can also be played utilizing the flannel board. Instead of yarn and construction paper, felt pieces can be employed.

Spell It

Using two colors of 9″×12″ construction paper, rule off 2″ squares. Make 50 squares of each color, one to represent beginning sounds and the other to represent ending sounds of words.

Some of the sounds that can be printed on the cards are:

—Beginnings—

b	cr	g	l	r	sp	w
bl	d	gl	m	s	str	v
br	dr	gr	n	sl	sm	sn
c	f	h	p	st	t	ch
cl	fr	j	pl	sh	th	fl
k	pr	sk	tr			

—Endings—

ake	ap	ail	ame
ay	ess	and	ar
all	ane	ain	ell
ang	een	ike	ad
an	at	ew	ip
ade	ill	ime	ick
ack	ide	in	ight
ate	ing	ink	ag
ind	amp	et	own
ank	ow	ock	ong
op	ook	ound	un
id	ace	ant	ed

Once the sounds are printed on the cards they can be laminated and cut.

To play:

This game can be played with two to eight players. The pieces are placed face down in a box or on the table. Each player chooses eight pieces to be seen only by him. The first player takes a sound card from his hand and places it face up on the table. The player on his right chooses a card from his hand and places it next to the first card to complete the word. If he does not have one, he is allowed three from the pile to try to finish the word. If he is unable to lay a card down, he passes, and the next player tries to complete it. After a word has been made, the next player starts a new one. The first player who uses all his cards wins.

Battle Stations

Materials needed:

1 colored oaktag board, 24″×36″
4 colors of construction paper

Making the board:

On the colored construction paper draw four circles, 9″ in diameter. Glue the circles in the corners of the oaktag board as shown in Figure 7-3.

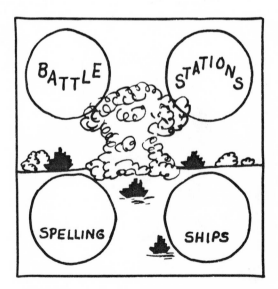

FIGURE 7-3: Battle Stations Game Board

Making the spinner:

Using heavy oaktag, cut a round spinner divided into four sections, each representing a color on the playing board. Cut an arrow from heavy poster board and attach it to the center of the spinner with a paper fastener.

Making the playing cards:

Using one color of 9″×12″ construction paper, rule off 3″×2″ sections. Write words from your spelling book on these cards. Then laminate and cut the cards.

Making the navy:

On a ditto make about 30 navy ships to be used as game tokens. Run off two sheets of ships for each color on the playing board. Laminate and cut them out.

To play:

This game is designed for four players. Each player chooses his battle station and places eight of his ships on it. The cards are placed face down in the middle of the board. The first player spins the spinner to find out whom he attacks. If the arrow points to his own color, he spins again. The first player then chooses a card and reads it to his opponent. If the opponent spells the word correctly, he gets to place another ship from his surplus navy on his battle station. If he spells it incorrectly, he must give one of his ships from his battle station to the attacker. If the attacker can not read the word, he gives the card to the opponent to read. If the opponent reads it, the attacker must give one of his ships to that player. When neither the attacker or the opponent can read the word it is placed in the sunken ship pile. The winner of the game is the player who has the strongest or largest navy on his battle station.

Drag Race

Materials needed:

24″×24″ poster board
construction paper
4 tokens

Making the board:

On poster board, make a speedway as shown in Figure 7-4.

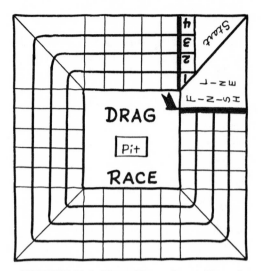

FIGURE 7-4: Drag Race Game Board

Making the game cards and tokens:

Rule off the construction paper into $3'' \times 3''$ blocks. Write spelling words and a number from 1 to 6 in these blocks. Laminate and then cut them out.

To play:

The object of the game is to move all three cars to the finish line first. All players place their cars in position at their starting line. The first player draws a card from the pit, reads the word, and then gives its definition. If all players agree with this definition, he moves forward the number of spaces designated on the card. If not, he moves back the same number.

Concentration

Materials needed:

construction paper, 2 colors
card holder

Making the cards:

Rule off $4'' \times 3''$ blocks on each color of construction paper. You will need 30 blocks of each color. On one color number from 1 to 30. On the other color, write 15 spelling words, using the other 15 to write the definitions.

Shuffle the word and definition cards and place them at random in the card holder, face up. Cover these cards with the numbered cards in sequence.

To play:

The object of the game is to match the spelling word with its definition. The player removes two of the numbered cards. If he uncovers a word and its definition, he keeps the match. If they do not match, the numbered cards are replaced and the next player takes his turn. The player with the most matches at the end of the game wins.

Spelling Darts

Materials needed:

suction cup darts
chalkboard

To play:

Draw on the chalkboard a target giving each section a number. The caller reads a word to be spelled by the player. If he spells it correctly, he throws three darts and adds up his score. If he doesn't spell the word correctly, he does not throw the darts. Play is continued, adding each score to the player's previous total. The winner can be determined either by being the first to reach the set goal or by having the highest score at the end of a given time period.

PAPER GAMES

Initial Dot:

On a sheet of paper make six rows of dots with six dots in each row. One player reads a spelling word to his opponent. If the opponent spells the word correctly, he connects any two dots with a line segment in a horizontal or vertical manner. If he misspells the word he cannot connect any dots. Play continues back and forth between the two players. Each time a player connects two dots which close a square, he puts his initial in it. The object of the game is to win the most squares.

Spelling Designs:

This game is intended for four to five players. One player draws a design covering a sheet of drawing paper. Each player has a different color crayon to use throughout the game. The first player reads a word to be spelled by the second player. If he spells it correctly, he colors in one section of the design. The players continue in the same manner in turn. When all sections of the design have been colored, the player with the most colored portions wins.

How Many? ✓

The object of this activity is to make as many words as possible from one long word. The letters can be used only the number of times they appear in the word. Some words that can be used for this activity are:

Rumplestiltskin	Mother Goose	Circumference	Memorial Day
Encyclopedia	London Bridge	Manufacturers	Mathematics
George Washington	Hippopotamus	Electronics	White House
Merry Christmas	Elephants	Astrology	Pocahontas
Czechoslovakia	Cafeteria	Television	Shakespeare
Captain Blue Beard	Chevrolet	Santa Claus	Michelangelo
Abraham Lincoln	Reservation	Netherlands	Combinations
Valentine's Day	California	Rhinoceros	Chemistry
Christopher Columbus	Repairman	Elementary	Popsicles
United Nations	Magazines	Gymnasium	Arrangements
Vice-President	Presentation	Oldsmobile	Pennsylvania
Refrigerators	Halloween	Telephones	Mountainside
Atlantic Ocean	Veterans' Day	Orthodontist	Automobiles
New Hampshire	Spaghetti	Description	Adolescence
Chrysanthemum	Clam Chowder	Apartments	Tobogganing
Massachusetts	Languages	Locomotive	Switzerland
Transportation	Presidential	Thanksgiving	Expressway

Dictionary Search ✓

To familiarize the children with the format of dictionaries and the information they contain, we write on numbered oaktag cards different activities dealing with the dictionary. Some of the activities could be:

1. Find twenty abbreviations.
2. Find ten contractions and the words they stand for.
3. Find twenty compound words.
4. Find three words for each of the prefixes. (List them.)
5. Find three words for each of the suffixes.
6. Find twenty 3-syllable words.
7. Find twenty 4-syllable words.
8. Find twenty 5-syllable words.

9. Find twenty words with double consonants.
10. Find twenty words with double vowels.
11. Find twenty words with four different meanings.
12. Find an action word for every letter of the alphabet.
13. Find a noun for every letter of the alphabet.
14. Find a describing word for every letter of the alphabet.
15. Find the name of an animal for every letter of the alphabet.
16. Find a name of a food for every letter of the alphabet.
17. Find an occupation for every letter of the alphabet.
18. Find one long "a" word for every letter in the alphabet.
19. Find one long "e" word for every letter.
20. Find one long "i" word for every letter.
21. Find one long "o" word for every letter.
22. Find one long "u" word for every letter.
23. Find one short "a" word for every letter.
24. Find one short "e" word for every letter.
25. Find one short "i" word for every letter.
26. Find one short "o" word for every letter.
27. Find one short "u" word for every letter.
28. Find twenty words that can be used as both a noun and a verb.
29. Find twenty words and their plurals.
30. Find twenty words with capital letters.

Each child makes a "dictionary diary." When a child chooses one of the listed cards, he writes the number and the activity at the top of one of his pages in his diary, and then proceeds to do the activity. Next to each word he records the number of the page he found the word on.

8

Sight and Sound Experiences Through the A. V. Shop

Sight and sound activities through the use of audio visual materials provide an excellent way of reinforcing skills and concepts relating to all areas of knowledge. The audio visual equipment is not limited to this shop; it is used extensively in all the other shops. The A.V. activities in the other shops can be used for this shop if so desired. These activities are explained in detail in the other chapters. In this chapter we will discuss the activities that are of a general nature.

The equipment and supplies in this shop are:

record player	filmstrips
tape recorder	records
filmstrip viewer	films
overhead projector	transparencies
film projector	construction paper
headphone set	newsprint
slide projector	magazines and newspapers
opaque projector	projection pens
cassettes	

SCRAPBOOKS

Children are fascinated by the collecting and categorizing of objects. One way to capture this enthusiasm is to have them create their very own scrapbooks.

Allow the children to choose a topic that excites them. Some suggestions are:

zoo animals	beverages	farms
dogs	gems	pollution

insects	musical instruments	seasons of the year
flowers	emotions	leaves
food groups	water	cartoons
boats	state capitals	buildings
communication	outer space	sports
Indians	circus	universities
poems with pictures	appliances	rockets
trees	community business	country vs. city
clothing	cats	money
countries	birds	antiques
cars	sea animals	machines
holidays	houses	Armed Forces
occupations	airplanes	tools
famous people	trains	mining
dinosaurs	toys	U.F.O.'s
household items	monuments	carnivals
bridges	recipes	plants
museums	rocks	reptiles
government	postcards	

The scrapbooks the children make are composed of pictures and articles from newspapers, magazines, photographs, brochures, etc. Each entry should be labeled. This project is designed to cover a long period of time. The completed scrapbooks can be displayed in your classroom or library.

COMMERCIAL MATERIALS

Available to teachers are many materials which are ready for use in the A.V. Shop. Among these are:

> films
> filmstrips
> mathematical records
> records with accompanying books
> tapes
> phonics records
> listening records

Commercially prepared materials should not be the main substance of the A.V. Shop, but should be launching points for creative, child-oriented activities. Our audio visual shop encourages the philosophy of "hands on" experiences.

PICTURE COLLAGES

Collages give the children the opportunity to express their own ideas about a given topic. They arrange their collections of pictures and words from magazines and newspapers in an eye-catching display on poster board. Some topics that may interest the children are:

love	happiness	war	evil
sadness	green	heaven	sickness
beauty	orange	generosity	friendship
yellow	blue	work	silence
black	freedom	chaos	sounds
red	defeat	conflicts	contrasts
pride	confidence	determination	power
success	death	compassion	time
peace	prayer	memories	talent
fear	summer	excitement	anticipation
winter	spring	fall	
hate	loyalty	courage	

CARTOON FINALE

Developing logical sequences of events and drawing your own conclusions are important facets in the listening skills of storytelling. To help achieve these goals the children listen to records of stories or cassette tapes the teacher has prepared. The story is stopped at a climactic point and the children record their own interpretation of the subsequent events on at least four frames of a cartoon strip.

STORYTELLING TAPES

The focus of these tapes is on originality and creativity in developing a make-believe story. Working in pairs, the children compose holiday stories centered around these topics:

HALLOWEEN:

The Witch That Lost Her Broom	The Witch's Brew
The Goblin on Green Street	The Black Cat Caper
Ghosts Galore	The Ghostly Trio
Pumpkin Eaters	The Haunting Shadow

THANKSGIVING:

The Pilgrim's Problem
The Tasteless Turkey
The Indian that Came to Dinner
The Turkey Trot

The Turkey That Said No
The Cranberry Patch
Gone with the Wind

CHRISTMAS:

Christmas Away from Home
The Reindeer Who Broke His Leg
Santa's Workshop
Snowbound
Heat Wave at the North Pole
The Candy Cane Factory
The Jingling of the Bells
The Caroler Who Couldn't Sing

The Littlest Christmas Present
The Tallest Christmas Tree
Santa's Helpers
The Unexpected Visitors
The Broken Toys
Anticipation on Christmas Eve
The Singing Stocking

VALENTINE'S DAY:

The Broken Heart
The Candy Hearts
Valentine Fever
My Secret Valentine

Valentine Party
The Talking Heart
The Land of Valentine People

PRESIDENTS' DAY:

The Day Honest Abe Wasn't Honest
Why George Washington Chopped Down the Cherry Tree
A Day in the Life of George Washington
George Washington's First Press Conference
The Assassination of Abraham Lincoln
The President's Day
The Night Before Election

ST. PATRICK'S DAY:

The Happy Shamrock
The Luck of the Irish
The Pot of Gold
The Leprechaun Dance
"Top o' the Mornin' to You!"

The Four Leaf Clover Story
The Lost Leprechaun
Who Found the Leprechaun's Hat
Why the Leprechaun Has Curly Toes
Why the Irish Like Green

APRIL FOOLS:

Why April 1st Is Fools Day   The Frightening Trick
The Fool That Fooled Himself   Why the Fool Cried
The Funny Trick

EASTER:

Easter Magic   The Jumping Jelly Beans
Scrambled Eggs   The Easter Parade
The Bunny Who Couldn't Hop   The Missing Easter Basket
The Hidden Easter Present   The Easter Bonnet
The Egg Hunt

MEMORIAL DAY:

The Memorial Day Parade   The War That Nobody Started
The Rained-Out Parade   The Shiny Uniform
The Tomb of the Unknown Soldier The Too-Small Uniform
The War That Wasn't Won   The Torn Flag
The Memorial Day Picnic

NEWSPAPER PRINT POSTERS

A unique follow-up to a film, record, or filmstrip, and one that allows a child to express a main idea, is the *newspaper print poster*. This project develops word recognition and creative expression. After the child reviews the material, he chooses a picture from a magazine or newspaper that depicts the main idea. He then proceeds to write a short paragraph explaining the importance of the picture, using words he locates in a newspaper or magazine. He cuts these words out and pastes them on the poster along with his picture.

COLORING BOOKS

A service project the children find interesting is making coloring books for younger children. The group decides upon a theme or title for their book. With pencils, the children draw simple pictures on 8½" by 11" white paper, and then print captions under each. Then they trace over all pencil marks with black Magic Marker, and compile the drawings in a book, complete with a title. The children achieve a great sense of satisfaction as they watch the enjoyment younger children have coloring the pictures.

CAREER CARDS

The Career Education program is growing in significance in the schools today, and an activity that builds up interest in this program is the Career Card File. On 5″ by 7″ unlined file cards, write occupational titles such as dentist, banker, geologist, astronomer, architect, archeologist, congressman, lawyer, accountant, optician, etc. These cards are filed alphabetically. The child chooses an occupation and writes a brief description of the job on a lined 5″ by 7″ card. On the reverse side of that card he draws a picture illustrating it. He then files this card behind the title card. Using the information from his card he can make a transparency or slide to serve as an aid in informing the group about the particular occupation. Allow only one job description for each title card so that the children can explore all types of work and get a better understanding of the world around them.

STORYTIME CREATIONS

The emphasis in this activity is on personification. The group chooses a title card and writes a story about it, making sure the object in the title is brought to life. For example, under the title, "How the Shoe Got Its Hole," the story might begin as follows:

> It was dark in the cramped closet. Suddenly the sunlight streamed in as Bobby opened the door. Oh boy! He's going to put me on today. I wonder where we are going. Oh no! He's taking me right through that snowdrift. Brrrr! It's cold. Help! I can't breathe! . . .

After the story is completed, the children draw a series of individual pictures to accompany the story. A small piece of flannel may be glued on the back so that pictures are usable on the flannel board.

The children tape the story they wrote in play form, with one child acting as narrator and the others as the objects and people.

The final step is the group's presentation of the taped story and flannel board pictures. To elaborate on the presentation, a visual "T.V." box (Figure 8-1) can be made to show the pictures. It can be constructed by following this procedure:

Using a large box, cut a 8″ by 10″ hole out of the bottom of the box. Drill two holes on each of the two long sides, approximately 1½″ from the ends of the box. Place two snug-fitting dowel rods through these holes, letting them extend at least 2″ on the outside of the box. At the ends of the rods on one side, attach crank type handles. Then paint the box.

FIGURE 8-1: T.V. Box

The "film" for the "T.V." box is segments of white construction paper taped together to make a long roll. Tape the end of the paper roll to one of the rods inside the box. Then roll the paper around the rod and tape the other end of the paper roll to the second rod. When you turn one of the handles on the box, your "T.V. story" will unfold like a filmstrip.

Some titles to develop the concept of personification are:

The Jealous Jellybean

The Fat Banana

The Paper Boots

The Drowning Ship

The Hard Life of the Highway

The Trampled Doormat

The Blues of a Broom

Cookie Jar Caper

The Counterclockwise Clock

The Flighty Flute

The Potato's Great Escape

The Headaches of a Cymbal

The Hammer That Always Missed

Why the Sun Disappeared at Noon

The Airplane That Forgot How to Land

A Jacket's Visit to the Lost and
   Found Department

The Monotonous Life of a Stapler

The Babbling Brook

The Mitten Museum

A Day in the Life of a Finger

Shopping Cart Race Track

The Bursting Raincloud

My Feelings as a Wastebasket

The Record That Got Dizzy

Ouch! Cried the Glue Bottle

My Experiences as a Flat Tire

The Sassy Saxaphone

The Delirious Drum

The Vacuum Cleaner's Stomach Ache

The Career Possibilities of an Egg

What a Flower Thinks About
   All Day

The Bouncing Basketball That Won
   the Game

CARICATURES

This activity emphasizes listening for details by transforming taped descriptions into caricatures. Prepare tapes describing in vivid terms the characteristics of people. The children listen to the tape, and then each one draws a caricature. After the caricatures are finished, the children share them with each other, pointing out the details mentioned on the tape. The tape is then played over, and the children choose which caricature includes the most characteristics from the tape.

An example of a taped description is the following:

> Down by the sea lived an old, old sailor. He had black bulging eyes with dark circles underneath. The top of his head was bald, with strands of gray hair flowing from the sides. Perched on top of his shiny head was a dirty white sailor's cap. He smiled with a crooked toothless grin. In the center of his face was a pear-shaped nose which seemed too big for his face. On his right cheek was a scar shaped like a half-moon, which he received while fighting pirates. His days are now filled with smoking his long curved pipe and gazing out to sea.

ANIMAL ANTHOLOGY

The success of this project depends upon the child's wild imagination. On 4½" by 3" pieces of construction paper draw unusual lines that would lend themselves to the beginning of an imaginary animal. Figure 8-2 shows a few examples.

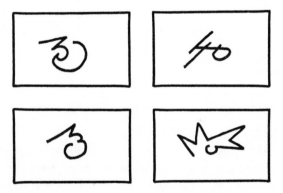

FIGURE 8-2: Sample Animal Anthology Cards

Children choose one of these cards and trace it on the tracing paper. Using their creative abilities the children develop their own unique animal. After the animal is colored, it is given a name and labeled as such. Tear the edges of the paper and mount on 9" by 12" construction paper. On a sheet of paper write an entry about the animal for the class anthology. The entry should include the following make-believe information:

—What are the habits of the animal?

—Where does it live? Describe its environment.
—Describe the home of your animal.
—What does it eat?
—Who are its enemies?
—How does your animal protect itself?
—How does your animal travel or move?

These entries are mounted on the reverse side of the mounted picture. The pictures and entries are then compiled into a class animal anthology.

Shop Around

Materials needed:

—two 30" by 20" poster boards
—colored construction paper
—transparencies
—diazo film and reversal film
—tape (cassettes)
—oaktag
—magazine pictures
—dice
—8 one-inch dowel rod sections for tokens
—6 baby food jars
—3" by 5" file cards
—overhead projector
—slide projector
—tape recorder

To make the board:

Design the Shop Around Game Board, using two 30" by 20" poster boards and the dimensions shown in Figure 8-3. Use a different color of construction paper to represent each one of the shops. Each one of the 6" by 4½" blocks stands for one of the shops, so make sure the construction paper color corresponds with the color of the shop. The 9" by 7" block represents the Consonant Blends Shop and thus both should be the same color of construction paper. Interspersed sparsely among the 1" squares are black dots which are made by using a paper punch. Label all the shops and the eight positions for START. Since the game board is so large it may be better to use Con-Tact paper to cover it instead of laminating paper.

To make the shopping tickets:

Using the same seven colors of construction paper for the seven shops, rule off 16 one-inch squares on each of the colors of paper. In every square

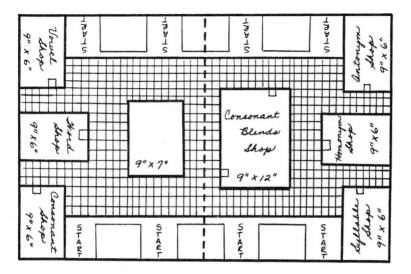

FIGURE 8-3: Shop Around Game Board

write the numbers 1, 2, 1, 2, etc., on all seven colors of paper. Laminate and cut. Place the numbered squares in seven baby food jars for storage.

To make the game cards:

Prepare eight game cards on 9" by 12" oaktag as shown in Figure 8-4.

To make the black dot direction cards:

On 3" by 5" index cards write the following list of directions:

—Go to the Antonym Shop.
—Take a shopping ticket from one of the players.
—Move three spaces in any direction.
—Give one of your shopping tickets to the player on your right.
—Take a shopping ticket from the player on your right.
—Send one of the players to a shop.
—Go to the Consonant Blends Shop.
—Go to the Homonym Shop.
—Miss one turn.
—Go back to start.
—Switch places with any player.

For each of the seven colors of construction paper make a direction card that says this: "Put one red shopping ticket back." Make duplicates of each of the above directions. Mount the direction cards on 4" by 6" sections of black construction paper and laminate.

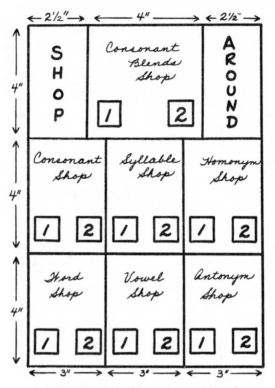

FIGURE 8-4: Shop Around Card

To make the activities in each shop:

1. *Consonant Shop.* Find pictures that stand for the beginning consonant sounds. Mount on the construction paper that is the same color as the shop and laminate.

2. *Syllable Shop.* Tape a variety of words with different numbers of syllables in them. Take about an eight-second pause between the words. Place a strip of construction paper the same color as the shop on the tape.

3. *Homonym Shop.* With a primary typewriter type homonym words. Below each set of homonym words type two sentences showing the meaning of the two words. If a diazo machine is available in your school system, make diazo transparencies for this shop. If not available make regular transparencies from the typed pages. Place on mounted frames and make windows for the set of homonym words and windows for the set of sentences. An example of what a homonym transparency would look like follows:

threw   through

Don *threw* the ball to his friend.
The ball went *through* the window.

knot   not

The sailor made a tight *knot* on the rope to hold the sail in place.
I am *not* doing the right job.

one   won

She has *one* good friend.
We *won* the ball game.

wood   would

The *wood* was placed in the fireplace.
We *would* like to go to the fair.

A suggested list of other homonym words that can be used are:

main—mane	red—read	knew—new
there—their	tied—tide	write—right
night—knight	bare—bear	bee—be
I—eye	hour—our	ate—eight
pane—pain	pair—pear	see—sea
tale—tail	heel—heal	rode—road
blew—blue	hear—here	sale—sail
meat—meet	plane—plain	buy—by
beat—beet	witch—which	sent—cent
weak—week	two—too	made—maid
pale—pail	sun—son	dear—deer
seem—seam	dew—do	wait—weight

4. *Word Shop*. This shop contains homemade slides using diazo film and oaktag strips as explained in the Science Shop chapter. Using dry transfer letters, write words from the Dolch basic sight vocabulary list on each slide.

5. *Vowel Shop*. Rule off 4½″ by 3″ blocks on the colored paper that is the same color as the shop. Using dry transfer letters, write in the blocks the different vowels and vowel combinations with an example word like these:

long A—ate	long E—me	long I—night
long O—no	long U—use	short A—apple
short E—net	short I—Indian	short O—octopus
short U—umbrella	oo—school	ow—blow
oa—boat	oy—boy	ou—out
oo—book	Y as in *baby*	Y as in *my*
C-V-C-E—kite	oe—toe	ie—tie
ea—beat	oi—soil	aw—saw
au—caught	ee—see	ay—say
	ai—wait	

6. *Antonym Shop.* On 4½″ by 2″ blocks of construction paper the same color as that of the shop, write words for which a child can give antonyms. A suggested list of antonym words is:

cold	hot	active	lazy	go	stop
win	lose	top	bottom	happy	sad
wild	tame	black	white	on	off
open	close	asleep	awake	old	young
fix	break	cool	warm	empty	full
slow	fast	far	near	winter	summer
sour	sweet	come	leave	answer	question
short	tall	soft	hard	yes	no
well	sick	out	in	over	under
slow	quick	worse	better	ashamed	proud
loser	winner	early	late	false	truth
boy	girl	love	hate	lie	true
odd	even	sell	buy	wise	foolish
dirty	clean	fat	thin	small	large
untidy	neat	borrow	lend	good	bad
strong	weak	frown	smile	inside	outside
start	finish	old	new	last	first
peace	war	enemy	friend	wet	dry
day	night	ugly	pretty	down	up
noisy	quiet			big	little

7. *Consonant Blends Shop.* The media used in this shop are a set of thermal transparencies using cartoon characters as the motivating factor with several words around the character displaying the consonant blend. Included in the transparency is a balloon indicating the consonant blend being shown by the cartoon character.

For example, a cartoon character can be climbing a tree. The balloon can say: "Higher! I've got to get those *BR* words." Place the following *BR* words in the tree: brave, brown, brush, bright, brought. Make transparencies for each consonant blend. Some consonant blends that can be used are:

sk	sp	sc	br	str	wr	bl	ng
cl	cr	dr	fl	st	sl	tr	sh
ch	ph	wh	gl	pr	pl	sw	sm
			th	thr	fr	gr	

Preparing the playing board:

Each player places his token on the START of his choice. Each player is given a game card. Place the black direction cards on the block next to the

Consonant Blends Shop in the middle of the board. Put the Word Shop slides in the slide projector; Syllable Shop tape in the tape recorder; and the rest placed face down in their respective shops on the board. Set up the overhead projector to be used during the course of the game.

To play the game:

The object of the game is to go to all the shops. At each one the player must do the designated activity, thus earning shopping tickets to be placed on his game board which he must fill up in order to win the game.

The first player rolls the dice and moves toward a shop. The players do this in turn until a player enters a shop. At this time the player does the designated activity for that shop. The activities that must be completed for each shop are as follows:

1. Consonant Shop—Say the picture and think of another word with the same beginning consonant sound.
2. Syllable Shop—Listen to *one* word on the tape recorder; say it and tell how many syllables are in that word.
3. Homonym Shop—Place the transparency on the overhead; flip one window frame over, showing one set of homonym words and two sentences. Say the two words; read the two sentences; then tell what each homonym word means.
4. Word Shop—Read the word that is on the slide in the slide projector.
5. Vowel Shop—Draw a vowel card; read the vowel or vowels and the word; then think of another word with the same vowel sound in it.
6. Antonym Shop—Choose an antonym card; read the word and give its opposite.
7. Consonant Blends Shop—Place one transparency on the overhead and read all the words on it.

When a player completes the activity of the shop correctly, he takes a shopping ticket of the same color as the shop and places it on his game board. Every player must go to all the shops two times in order to fill his game card and become the winner. When any player lands on a square with a black dot he must draw a black direction card and do what it says. Players continue playing the game in this fashion until a player has his game card filled up with shopping tickets, two from every shop. He is then declared the winner.

9

Becoming Aware of the World in the Social Studies Shop

The total growth and development of a person includes an awareness of the world about him. The activities found in our Social Studies Shop provide involvement in geography, people, events and issues both past and present, world organizations, and systems of government. Some units we have explored in our shop are:

Maps	Oceans
Indians	Seven Wonders of the World
Pollution	Transportation
Ships	Government
United Nations	Presidents
Alaska	Communication
United States	Space and Astronauts
Civil War	Deserts

To give you an idea of some of the activities found in the shop, the following units will be discussed in detail:

Indians
United Nations
Alaska
Ships

UNIT DEVELOPMENT

The environment of the shop reflects the unit being studied. Found there is a supply of resource books, charts, and diagrams relating to the unit of concentration. The children are also encouraged to contribute materials for display. Most unit work in the shops is done by partners. Each set of partners is given a packet which contains all the information they need. The front page of the packet lists the activities that must be completed. The subsequent pages describe the activities in more detail. It's a good idea to have all the materials needed for the unit activities, such as construction paper, drawing paper, etc., in the shop ahead of time.

INDIAN STUDY

This Indian study emphasizes the artistic aspect of Indians of long ago.

Activity 1: Indian Way of Life

To introduce the Indian way of life, a picture book of Indians motivates a discussion. Some of the points that should be stressed during the course of the discussion are:

> teepees
> totem poles
> buffalo
> grizzly bears
> war dances
> kachina dolls
> Indian children's toys and games
> implements such as clubs, scalp sticks,
>> beaver traps, prayer sticks, moccasins,
>> bows and arrows, etc.

After the discussion, the children make a large picture depicting one of the facets of Indian life.

Activity 2: Indian Designs

A characteristic of Indian work is the use of colorful designs in their pottery, jewelry, weaving, and teepees. In this activity the children create a design on black paper with paint.

Activity 3: Picture Writing

Display a chart of Indian picture writing, showing both the symbols and what each stands for, or have books available with the same information. The children practice drawing the symbols. On construction paper and using the picture language they then write a message to Sitting Bull.

Activity 4: Sand Art

On 6" by 6" pieces of paper, the children draw a simple Indian design. Spread glue along the lines, one line at a time. Sprinkle sand or corn meal over the glue. Let the glue dry, and then shake off the excess particles carefully. If you want your design to be colored, add food coloring to the sand or corn meal. Display all the designs on a bulletin board to make one large Indian design collage.

Activity 5: Dance Steps

Books showing Indian dance steps and sign language are necessary for this activity. Working in partners, practice the various dance steps and then make up a dance to be shown to the other members of the group.

Activity 6: Sign Language

Using their hands, the children practice the sign language the Indians used for communication. They make up a sentence transferring the words into sign language. The other children try to guess what the sentence is about.

Activity 7: Totem Pole

The children practice one face that they want to draw for their group's totem pole. They draw the figure on graph paper, using Magic Markers, colored chalk, or crayons. Then they cut their pictures out and hang them on top of each other to make a group totem pole.

A variation of this activity is the making of a plaster totem pole. Mix the plaster according to directions. Pour it into the milk cartons the children have saved from their lunches. When the plaster has hardened, peel the carton off. Using scissors, carve the face. Paint and assemble on top of each other. To preserve these, coat with shellac.

Activity 8: Tribal Picture Book

The partners choose one of the following Indian tribes to research:

Navaho	Iroquois
Apache	Souix
Hopi	Seminole
Chippewa	Cherokee

The following information should be included in their research:

1) Where the tribe lived in the United States.
2) Any famous leaders of the tribe: who they are; what they did.
3) Tribe characteristics.
4) Who their enemies were, if any.

5) Meaning of the tribe name.

6) Physical features and dress.

This information will be compiled in a group book which will include pictures and reports.

Activity 9: Indian Stamping Grounds

Each set of partners receives a ditto map of the U.S.A. On this map they are to show where each of the Indian tribes lived. At that location, they draw a small characteristic feature of that tribe. They label it.

Using a transparency of the U.S., project the outline on a large sheet of paper and trace. This outline should be large enough to cover a full bulletin board. Choose a child to draw a doll and dress it to represent one of the tribes and place in the proper location on this bulletin board. Label the tribe; do this for the other seven tribes.

Activity 10: Indian Villages

Working as a group, the children will make a display on a table of one of the following types of Indian Villages:

> Indians of the Desert
> Indians of the Woodlands
> Indians of the Plains

The table displays should include the following:

1) the physical environment of the area

2) type of houses

3) working implements

4) mode of travel

5) Indians themselves.

UNITED NATIONS

The objective of this unit is to help the children understand the importance of the United Nations as an organization designed to achieve international cooperation and develop friendly relations among nations for world peace.

The activities in this unit incorporate many of the subject areas such as language, letter writing, geography, researching, art, role-playing, choral reading, and music.

Activity 1: Introduction

In order to arouse interest, read a book or show a film to the class about the United Nations. Then discuss with the class the fact that each child will become a delegate representing one of the countries in the United Nations. Either allow the children to choose a country or assign a country to them.

Activity 2: Letter Writing

To help the make-believe delegates to assume their roles more effectively, letters can be written to the embassies requesting information about their country. A list of embassy addresses can be found in your library in the New York City Telephone Directory.

Activity 3: Flags

The children will practice drawing on newsprint the flag representing their country. In their practice drawing they must make their flag cover the entire paper, concentrating on exact placement of symbols and the appropriate colors. After practicing, the final design is drawn on 9" by 12" manila oaktag and then painted.

Activity 4: Maps

On colored construction paper the children will trace the outline of the continent in which their country is located and trace the outline of their country within that continent. Both the continent and the country are then labeled.

Activity 5: Dolls

This activity requires the children to obtain pictures illustrating their country's native costume. These pictures can be found in magazines, encyclopedias, books, place mats, etc.

Once the picture has been secured, the children trace the pattern of a doll on both sides of a piece of drawing paper. The doll pattern looks like Figure 9-1.

The children color the front of the costume on one side of the drawing paper and the back of the costume on the reverse side. After this has been completed, the pattern is traced on manila oaktag and cut out. The clothing is made from colored construction paper and glued on the doll. Using 12" by 1" strips of white paper, folded in half, write the name of the country on the front and back. Place the costume on the doll as shown in Figure 9-2. The finished dolls can be suspended from the ceiling.

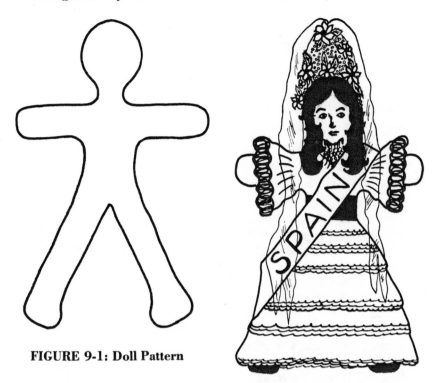

FIGURE 9-1: Doll Pattern

FIGURE 9-2: Costumed Doll

Activity 6: Small Group Projects

To enlighten the children on some of the many facets of the U.N., they will be divided into small groups and assigned one of the following projects:

Project A: Special Reports

Within this group the children can explore the following topics:

League of Nations
Main bodies
 —General Assembly
 —Security Council
 —Secretariat
 —Economic and Social Council
 —Trusteeship Council
 —International Court of Justice
How to become a member.
Secretary Generals of the U.N.
Art and sculpture in the U.N. building.

How to become a guide in the U.N. building.
What the U.N. flag stands for.
Information about the Secretariat building.
Draw the U.N. building and locate the agencies, using a floor plan.

Project B: Agency Murals

The children research the various agencies of the United Nations. They must find the symbol for the agencies and the type of work they do for the world. The murals depict the symbol, the title, and a representative picture of each agency's job. Some agencies of the U.N. are:

International Labor Organization (ILO)
Food and Agriculture Organization (FAO)
World Health Organization (WHO)
United Nations Educational, Scientific, and Cultural Organization (UNESCO)
International Atomic Energy Agency (IAEA)
International Bank
International Telecommunication Union (ITU)
World Meteorological Organization (WMO)
International Civil Aviation Organization (ICAO)
International Finance Corporation (IFC).

Project C: U.N. in the News

Using newspapers and weekly news magazines, the children create a scrapbook of articles pertaining to the U.N. and its activities. Each article should be accompanied by the source, the date, and a short review of what it's about. If desired, this activity can be expanded by conducting an opinion poll on selected questions about the articles or soliciting general reactions to the articles.

Project D: International Picture Bulletin Board

To emphasize the U.N.'s ideal objective of working for the betterment of all the people of the world, a picture collage bulletin board can be designed. This collage should include pictures showing people helping people, nations helping nations, and the U.N. maintaining peace among countries. A good title or theme for this collage is "U.N. in Action."

Activity 7: Research

As a delegate to the United Nations, each child is responsible for learning as much as he can about his country. He can accumulate this information either from literature he received from his embassy or reference books in the library. Some facts he should include in his report are:

1) date of entrance into the U.N.

2) main occupation of the people
3) population
4) language spoken
5) type of houses they live in
6) typical mode of dress
7) games they play or the favorite sport
8) favorite or most popular food.

Activity 8: International Cookbook

Using the research as a source, the children write down on newsprint a recipe including the popular food of the country. With this recipe include a picture drawing of the dish. The child transfers the recipe and drawing onto a ditto master. Enough copies are made of each recipe to make an international cookbook for each child.

Activity 9: World Bulletin Board

To illustrate the vast area the U.N. affects, a world map is drawn on the bulletin board with the aid of an overhead projector. Each child will draw and color a small replica of the flag representing his country on 1½" by 2" white construction paper. Using a straight pin, place the flags on the map to label the countries. Pull the flag to the head of the pin.

Activity 10: Culminating Activity

Since October 24 is the birthday of the United Nations, an excellent culminating activity for the entire class would be to salute the U.N. with a program—including a mock general assembly.

Preparation for the program:

1. Elect or choose a president, a secretary-general, and an executive assistant to preside over the program.

2. In the background display the flags the children made in alphabetical order. In the center of the flags of the countries display the United Nations flag.

3. All the delegates wear a paper headband six inches high with the name of their countries lettered across it. During the program, the delegates will be seated in alphabetical order according to countries.

4. Place on the center stage three desks, attaching the following name cards: (1) Secretary-General, (2) President, (3) Executive Assistant. Also have a podium and a public address system to one side of the front part of the stage.

5. The delegates' chairs are placed in three sections facing the stage, as in the real United Nations Assembly.

Events in the U.N. Program:

The program basically consists of two parts: (1) the General Assembly, and (2) some selected songs, poems, and choral readings about the U.N. itself or related goals. The songs, poems, and choral readings can be made up by the children, or they can be found in books. They can be used for an introduction to the general assembly as well as a closing.

The following could be the procedure to follow for a Mock General Assembly:

1. The President would call the Assembly to order and ask the Secretary General to take the roll call. As the names of the countries are called in alphabetical order, the delegates file up to the podium and announce that their country is present. At this time they will also state an interesting fact about their country that they found out as a result of their research.

2. The President calls upon the delegates who have special reports to come to the podium to present them to the assembly.

3. The President informs the assembly of a problem. There can then be an open debate on this problem or the delegates can prepare speeches to support both sides of the issue. After the problem has been discussed thoroughly, the Secretary General calls each country in alphabetical order and the delegates stand and declare their votes. The votes can be either "Yes," "No," or "Abstain." The Secretary General tabulates these votes and passes the decision on to the President who then anounces the results to the Assembly.

Delegate Etiquette:

1. All delegates stand when officers enter and depart.
2. During roll call delegates answer like this: "_____is present."
3. During voting, the delegates respond like this: "_____votes yes."
4. Executive Assistant directs the singing.

We found this to be an exciting and powerful unit. The intense enthusiasm and cooperation that begins to build from the letter writing activity shines through in the culmination activity. The final program actually proves to be a moving and exhilarating experience for the spectators as well as for the participants.

ALASKA

Our 49th state provides an interesting focal point for a unit of study. The fact that it holds such fascination and mystery lends itself to an inspiring unit for the children to investigate.

The development of this unit consists of two main parts—scrapbooks and group projects. Each set of partners completes a scrapbook of Alaska. The following information should be contained in the scrapbook:

1. *Map*—Outline the state of Alaska and locate the capital.
2. *Shelter*—Describe the shelter used in the past and the housing found in the present, both in rural and city areas. Draw pictures illustrating the three types.
3. *Transportation*—Draw pictures of the various kinds of transportation found in Alaska. Label each one.
4. *Foods*—Make a chart showing the main types of foods that are eaten.
5. *Climate*—Assuming the role of a meteorologist, show the temperatures of a summer day and a winter day in each of the following three regions: Southern region; Interior region; and the Northern region. To accurately show the temperatures make six thermometers and label each.
6. *Occupations and Industries*—Describe the various occupations and industries found in Alaska in order of importance.
7. *Population*—Find the total population of Alaska and the populations for the following cities: Anchorage, Fairbanks, Juneau, Ketchikan, Nome, Seward, and Palmer.
8. *Natural Resources*—List the natural resources and their locations.
9. *Dress*—Draw pictures showing seasonal dress of the Alaskans.
10. *Wildlife*—Write a report on the wildlife of Alaska and draw pictures to accompany the report.

After the scrapbooks have been completed, each group is assigned a culminating project which correlates with the ten previous activities. If your class is divided into less than ten groups, choose the projects you feel are most important. If you have twelve groups assign two groups to two of the more complex projects.

Project 1

Draw the outline of the state on a large plywood base. Fill in the outline with a salt ceramic dough. The following is a recipe you can use to make the dough:

> 1 c. salt
> ½ c. cornstarch
> ¾ c. water

Cook in an old pan until it forms a glob. Place the glob on wax paper until it is cool enough to handle, then knead it until it makes a nice smooth ball. Wrap the ball in Saran Wrap and then in foil until ready for use. Knead the ball again before using.

On painted popsicle sticks, write the names of the following cities and place them upright in their proper locations: Anchorage, Fairbanks, Juneau,

Ketchikan, Nome, Seward, Palmer, Kodiak, Fort Yukon, Wales, Barrow, Port Hope, and Unalaska. Use a special marker to denote the state capital. After the salt ceramic form has hardened, it may be painted.

Project 2

The children draw pictures depicting the differences between the types of housing the rural Alaskans lived in both in the past and in the present. With the pictures as guides, construct two dioramas using grocery boxes labeled "Past Rural Alaska" and "Present Rural Alaska." Materials that can be used for this project are:

sugar cubes	milk cartons
Styrofoam flakes	salt
cotton	

Project 3

Construct a table display showing the different modes of transportation used in Alaska either in the past or in the present. Place each mode of travel in its proper environment.

Project 4

Taking on the role of a restaurant owner, prepare a menu found in a typical Alaskan restaurant. Your menu should include a dish the children can prepare and bring in for sample tasting.

Project 5

On a large wall map of Alaska show the differences in the amount of rainfall, using a colored legend. The needed information can be found by reproducing an existing rainfall map.

Project 6

Make a chart showing the process by which a natural resource is changed into the final product. A good example of this is the process involved in the canning of salmon.

Project 7

Using graph paper, prepare a graph showing the population of at least seven cities. Develop a graph comparing the population of the cities in Alaska in 1950 and the present day. These graphs can be enlarged for bulletin board displays.

Project 8

This project requires the use of the salt ceramic recipe. Using a salt ceramic recipe, make another map of Alaska, building up the mountain ranges and depressing the river areas. This map can then be painted. From their research, the children can construct tokens to represent each of the natural resources; these tokens are then placed in their proper location on the map. For example, a token which represents the oil could be a miniature oil well. The tokens can be labeled if desired.

Project 9

Using the pictures showing the seasonal dress in the children's scrapbooks as a guide, draw two large murals depicting the summer and the winter attire of the Alaskans. This mural can be done on black paper and colored with chalk.

Project 10

Construct a table display of Alaskan wildlife using clay models. Situate each animal in its typical habitat.

All of these projects and their scrapbooks can be displayed at an Alaskan Fair. A good time to have this fair would be in January, to celebrate their statehood on January 3, 1959.

SHIPS

Imagine this:

> You are on board a ship and it's late at night. You're standing on the deck, searching for the stars that are hiding behind the clouds. Suddenly, you see the hull of a ship silently appear, and then just as silently vanish into nothingness. You——have just seen a ghost ship!

The suspense and interest created by the above reading is sure to captivate the children in the development of a ship unit. This unit utilizes ships as a guiding light in the learning of the world through its important ports. The activities in this unit can be in packet form with the exception of the Bon Voyage Party which will be explained in detail later.

Activity 1: Ghost Ships

There are many enchanting tales that can be found in books about ghost ships. Select one ghost ship story and relate the known details to the children. The children can then write a paragraph giving their ideas explaining the mysterious disappearance. Then they can discuss the various reactions.

Activity 2: Nautical Terms

To familiarize the children with the parts of ships and sailing terminology, a book entitled "What Every Good Sailor Should Know" can be made. Words such as the following can be included in these books:

aft	bulkhead	passageway	pilot
beam	deck	starboard	porthole
bridge	hatch	companionway	signal flags
cabin	hull	forecastle	stern
galley	ladder	halyard	wheel
hold	mast	cargo	gangplank
amidship	overhead	log	keel
bow	port	moorings	rigging

Activity 3: Murals

Four murals would be made illustrating the following titles:

1) Pleasure Crafts (rowboats, sailboats, canoes, cabin cruisers, ferry boats, etc.)
2) In the Harbor (tugboats, Coast Guard, fireboats, etc.)
3) Oceangoing Vessels (cargo ships, ocean liners, military ships, submarines, etc.)
4) Ancient Ships (Viking ships, schooners, clipper ships, etc.)

Each child chooses one of the four titles and, using available books, draws a corresponding picture. Make sure each group has at least one representative picture for each mural. From the drawings, the teacher selects two or three students to make each mural.

Activity 4: Model Ships and World Map

Divide the children into groups of three or four, designating one person as captain of the crew. Each crew devises the blueprint for their ship and gives it a name. One child from each crew makes a ship about 8″ long from a salt ceramic recipe. Toothpicks are handy for supporting the ship and for the masts of the ship. After the salt ceramic dries, the ship is painted and its name is painted on the bow.

The rest of the crew will color in the wall map of the world. This map is made by projecting the world image on white paper. Our map was projected on a gym wall and was approximately 8' by 12'. We labeled the continents, the oceans, and the following ports while it was on the wall:

New York, New York	Miami, Florida	Naples, Italy
Stockholm, Sweden	Kodiak, Alaska	Liverpool, England
Copenhagen, Denmark	Barcelona, Spain	Lisbon, Portugal
San Diego, California	Quebec, Canada	Hong Kong, China
Seattle, Washington	Honolulu, Hawaii	Havana, Cuba
Edinburgh, Scotland	Oslo, Norway	Bombay, India
Manila, Philippines	Portland, Maine	Tripoli, Africa
Halifax, Nova Scotia	Cape Town, Africa	Tokyo, Japan
San Francisco, California	Sydney, Australia	Bangkok, Thailand
Rio de Janeiro, Brazil	Athens, Greece	
San Juan, Puerto Rico	Casablanca, Africa	

Activity 5: Shipping Orders

Shipping orders for each ship include the home ports, the ports to be visited, and the information needed for each port. A sample shipping order would look like this:

SHIPPING ORDERS

To: Comanding Officer of the _____
  Home Port _____
From: Commander in Chief of All Ships
Orders: You are hereby directed to put the _____ to sea and set
  your course for the following ports:
  1. _____
  2. _____
  3. _____
Mission: Seek out and retain the following data from each port visited:
  1. city—things you find in city, places to see, interesting facts.
  2. weather and climate
  3. population
  4. religion
  5. transportation
  6. imports and exports

                                        Sincerely,

                                        Admiral Riggs
                                        Commander in Chief

The ports you assign each crew should be located in different parts of the world.

An effective way of giving out the shipping orders to the crews is to have a Bon Voyage Party. At the party, the shipping orders are given to each crew and are read by the captains. Each captain then places his ship at its home port on the world map, which is now lying on the floor at one end of the room. To increase the enthusiasm for the ship unit, the Bon Voyage Party can be made into a big production.

The crew members now have to complete the mission, finding the information for each port one at a time. After completing the first port, they move their ship to the second port and continue in the same fashion. The reports the crews make can include pictures and drawings as well. If a visual maker is readily accessible in your school, allow the crews to make a few slides of pictures from reference books about their ports.

After all the ships have returned to their home ports, the crews share their informations, pictures, and slides.

Activity 6: If I Could Sail Anywhere. . .

Each child chooses the two ports he would like to sail to, excluding the three ports his ship visited. On colored construction paper he draws pictures representing each port and writes the reason why he wants to sail there. This can be compiled into a class book entitled, "If I Could Sail Anywhere."

SOCIAL STUDIES LAB

The Social Studies Lab provides for further exploration in many of the vast areas dealing with Social Studies. The topics found at the stations enable the child to select one topic that he is interested in and to develop his own unit of study through the various activities offered.

The Lab is in operation between units (such as those previously mentioned in this chapter) and as a supplementary enrichment program for the children's use during their free time.

The Lab consists of five stations that deal with the same topics through specific activities. The children must follow through the five stations in order. The stations are:

Station One—films, filmstrips, slides, tapes, or records.
Station Two—titles to research.
Station Three—newspaper and radio station.
Station Four—activity cards.
Station Five—bonus activities: puzzles, questions to think about and answer, and games.

A detailed explanation of the stations, the materials needed, and some of the sample activities follow:

Station One

The materials needed at this station are any films, filmstrips, slides, tapes, or records that can be found dealing with each of the topics found in the Lab.

A slide presentation can be made, using one or two slides to represent each of the topics. After viewing this presentation, the children, working with their partners, can then decide which topic they wish to pursue at the other four stations.

Station Two

The necessary materials for this station are the report title cards, paper, and reference books. The partners choose a title from their topic that they would like to investigate. They should then do their research and prepare a report.

Some examples of report topics and corresponding titles are given here:

ASTRONAUTS AND SPACE
  Names of Astronauts
  Moon
  Gravity
  Cosmonaut
  Asteroids

DESERTS
  Sahara Desert
  Gobi Desert
  Death Valley
  Oasis

INDIANS
  All the Various Tribes
  Famous Indians
  Indian Terms

MAPS
  Hemisphere
  Longitude and Latitude
  Equator

OCEANOGRAPHY
  Jacques Cousteau
  Aqualung
  All Oceans of the World

PIONEER LIFE
  Pony Express
  Conestoga Wagon
  Buffalo Bill
  Davey Crockett

PREHISTORIC TIMES
  Dinosaurs
  Ice Age
  Fossil

SPORTS
  Names of Sports
  Names of Athletes

TRANSPORTATION
  Various Modes of Travel
  Famous Names in Transportation

WILD WEST
  Branding Iron
  Roundup
  Jesse James
  William G. Fargo

WORLD-WISE
  Cards of Continents—choose a
    country from that continent.

CALENDAR
  Holiday and Special Days
     of the Year

COMMUNICATION
  Radio
  Braille
  Alphabet
  Telegraph

HOBBIES
  Magic
  Coin Collecting
  Puppetry
  Pets

INVENTORS AND INVENTIONS
  Microscope
  James Watt
  Electric Light

MONEY
  Inflation and Deflation
  Federal Bank
  U.S. Mint

OUR COMMUNITY
  Post Office
  Hospital
  Police Station

PIRATES
  Libertatia
  "Black Bart"
  Captain Kidd

PRESIDENTS
  Names of Presidents
  Assassination
  Inauguration
  Impeachment

UNITED STATES
  50 States
  Betsy Ross
  Washington, D.C.
  White House

WONDERS AND MONUMENTS
  Stonehenge
  Statue of Liberty
  Mount Rushmore
  Grand Canyon

Station Three

Essentials needed at this station are:

—typewriter, if available
—pad of 18″ by 12″ newsprint, ruled off into three vertical columns
—date stamp
—paper strips cut 5″ wide in various lengths
—tape recorder

After researching at Station Two, the partners write a brief but complete news article based on that research. This is written or typed on the paper strips, and can then be mounted in the class newspaper. Each article must have a headline, and must include the names of the reporters. Before mounting anything, the first set of partners to use the newspaper must stamp (or print) the title of the paper on the top of the first sheet of newsprint. The date is then stamped underneath the title. Then the articles are mounted in one of the columns. Pictures may also be included with their articles. A new page is used each day for all the articles and pictures done at this station that day. If another page is needed for one day's work, stamp a second page and label it as such.

A tape recorder may also be found at this station. The partners may decide to make a news broadcast, or a commercial for the "radio" (which is the tape recorder) about their report.

Station Four

The activity cards found at this station require many different materials and tools, which can be found in the Handart Shop. A sample of some of the cards for each topic could be:

ASTRONAUTS AND SPACE
—Make a dictionary of "space" terms.
—Make a model of the earth and moon showing the spatial distance and the size difference.
—Create a crossword puzzle using space terms.
—Draw a picture of an astronaut in his spacesuit. Then design a spacesuit that could be used 100 years from now.
—Construct a model of a spaceship on its launching pad.

CALENDAR
—Make a diorama of the first Thanksgiving.
—Plan a Halloween Party; make invitations that you would send.
—Write a "Good Luck" story for St. Patrick's Day. Mount it on green construction paper shaped like a shamrock.

COMMUNICATION
—Make a chart of different types of communication.
—Make a chart of the Braille alphabet.
—Draw a diagram of a telegraph system.
—Make up your own code.

DESERTS
—Make a clay model of a desert animal.
—Make a picture book about "Life on a Desert."
—Make a table display of a desert.

HOBBIES
—If you could have a pet from anywhere in the world, what would you choose? Draw him.
—Make a puppet and write a play for your puppet.
—Start your own penny collection.

INDIANS
—Make an Indian headdress.
—Design a totem pole.

—Make an Indian tepee.

INVENTIONS AND INVENTORS

—List the five most important inventions in the world today.

—Choose one of the following "things" and draw a picture of what it would look like if you had invented it:

> A Gamwart
>
> A Fuselbuggy
>
> A Spatz

—Make a chart comparing a telescope and a microscope.

MAPS

—Draw a floorplan of the inside of your school building.

—Make a table display of a mini-town.

—Make a map of your mini-town.

—Make a treasure map.

—Using a map, plan a trip from your city to another city on the map.

MONEY

—Interview a person who works in a bank. Write about your interview.

—Design your own set of coins. Label the value of each.

—Make a chart showing some of the coins used in the United States.

OCEANOGRAPHY

—Draw a mural (chalk on blue paper) of the many things you would see underwater if you were a skin diver.

—Design an underwater city.

—Make a picture chart of the various shells found on a beach.

—Make a display of some clay ocean animals.

OUR COMMUNITY

—Make a picture book showing a policeman on various jobs.

—Make your own zoo chart. Color the animals first, cut, and mount on the chart.

—Make a diorama of some firemen on the scene of a fire.

—Make a paper doll and dress it to show the type of job you would like to do when you are older.

PIONEER LIFE

—Make a model of a mode of transportation used by the pioneers.

—Make a diorama of the inside of a pioneer home.

—Draw what the pioneer's dinner table might look like—the kind of food, type of utensils, etc.

—Make a large drawing showing a frontier settlement.

PIRATES
—Design a pirate ship. •
—Read the book, *Treasure Island,* by Robert L. /
"Wanted" poster for the pirate in that story.
—Read *Peter Pan* by James Barrie. Make a clay m.
pirate.

PREHISTORIC TIMES
—Make a collage divided into two parts depicting "Prehistoric Times" and "Today."
—Make a fossil.
—Suppose a full-sized dinosaur appeared on your street. Write and draw what might happen.

PRESIDENTS
—Make a mobile, using pictures of all the Presidents. Label each.
—Construct a model of the White House.
—Make an election poster that might have been used before one of the Presidents was elected.

SPORTS
—Make a dictionary of football terms.
—Make a comic book entitled "The Courageous Mountain Climber."
—Make a pictorial chart showing the development of the bicycle.
—Make a collage about outdoor sports.

TRANSPORTATION
—Experiment with different objects to see if they float in water. Chart your results.
—Make a picture chart of the development of the automobile.
—Make a scrapbook of the many ways to travel.
—Construct a model of a train.

UNITED STATES OF AMERICA
—Choose one of the 50 states and make a travel brochure for that state.
—Make a map of the U.S. and locate some famous points of interest.
—Create a crossword puzzle about the U.S.
—Find the importance of these U.S. symbols and draw a picture of each:

> Bald Eagle
> Uncle Sam
> Great Seal
> Statue of Liberty

WILD WEST
—Draw a saddle and label its parts.
—Make a poster advertising a rodeo.
—Make up a name for your ranch, then make up a branding symbol.
—Make up a comic strip about one of these characters:

> Annie Oakley
> Buffalo Bill
> Jesse James
> Calamity Jane
> "Wild Bill" Hickock

WONDERS AND MONUMENTS
—Make a model of a volcano. Draw a diagram of its inside.
—Make up some "What Am I?" riddles about some famous wonders or monuments.
—Make a clay model of Mt. Rushmore.

WORLD-WISE
—Make a flag of the country you researched, using a piece of material and magic markers.
—Choose a country from the address box and write a letter to that country requesting information.
—Make a travel log to show when and what you visited while traveling in a specific country.

Station Five

This station houses the bonus exercises. A file containing various puzzles and workbook pages are available for the children's enjoyment as a finale to their unit of study. In this file you may also want to include some interesting questions that the children will either have to think about or do research on in order to find the answers. Some of these puzzling questions could be:

Astronauts and Space: Why can't we always see the stars at night? Do stars actually twinkle?

Calendar: What is today's date? What interesting things happened on this day in history?

Deserts: Why is a camel a good desert animal?

Indians: What Indian tribe is represented on the U.S. nickel? Why?

Oceanography: Is there actually an underwater city called Atlantis? How do starfish move?

Presidents: Which President had the most children? How many did he have? Do you think a woman will ever be President of the U.S.? Explain.

The following games are also at this station. These games are easy to construct and are beneficial in emphasizing some Social Studies concepts.

Buried Treasure

This game emphasizes latitude and longitude concepts, and the directions of North, South, East, and West.

Materials needed:

20″ by 24″ poster board
18″ by 18″ piece of blue construction paper
9″ by 9″ poster board
4 one-inch length sections of dowel rods
1 paper fastener

How to make the board:

At one end of the board, measure a 20″ by 20″ square (see Figure 9-3). In the extra 4″ at the opposite end of the board write the name of the game. Center the 18″ by 18″ piece of blue construction paper in the 20″ square. Rule off the entire blue 18″ square into 1″ squares. Outline these squares with marker. Around the outside of the blue square, in the margin, write your latitude and longitude degrees, starting with 0 degrees at the center line on all sides, and increasing by 5 degrees at each line. Mount a 1½″-square

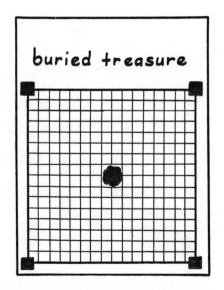

FIGURE 9-3: Buried Treasure Game Board

piece of construction paper in the center. A compass rose may be written on this to designate the directions for the board.

To make the spinner:

On the 9″ by 9″ poster board, draw an 8½″ diameter circle. Divide this into 12 pie-slice sections. On each of these sections, write one of these directions:

5 degrees North	10 degrees North	15 degrees North
5 degrees South	10 degrees South	15 degrees South
5 degrees East	10 degrees East	15 degrees East
5 degrees West	10 degrees West	15 degrees West

Next, make a 3″ arrow, and after laminating or covering the spinner and arrow with Con-Tact paper, attach the arrow to the board with the paper fastener.

To make the tokens:

Simply paint each of the tokens a different color for each player.

How to play the game:

The object of the game is to try to be the first to reach the island in the center of the board where the Buried Treasure is. Each player starts at his home base, one of which is in each of the four corners of the playing board.

The first player spins the spinner, and moves his token in the appropriate direction. For example, if the spinner lands on "5 degrees South" the player must move in a southerly direction from his place to the next line. If a player spins a northern direction and he cannot move, he remains there and skips his turn. When a player lands on a space occupied by his opponent, the opponent is sent back to his home base, to start again. The first player to land exactly on the island wins the game.

All Around Town

This game emphasizes the children's ability to read and interpret a pictorial legend on a map. A strong emphasis is also placed on their ability to follow the directions of North, South, East, and West.

Materials needed:

20″ by 30″ poster board
2 one-inch cubes

5 tokens of different colors

22″ by 18″ gray construction paper

How to make the board:

Mount the 22″ by 18″ gray construction paper at one end of the poster board, leaving margins as shown in Figure 9-4. Rule off the construction paper into 1″ squares, and outline the squares with black marker.

On different colors of construction paper, cut out ten small buildings to symbolize specific places around a town, such as a school, a hospital, a city park, a city hall, library, etc. Make sure each of these buildings is different from the others. Most of the buildings should be 1″ square so that they can fit inside the squares of the playing board. A few of them, such as the city park, may be larger. Make and cut out *three* of *each* building. Mount only one of each in various places on the board.

In the 8″ at the top of the board, label the game board and include a legend for the map of the town. In this legend, use the second set of your 1″ square buildings and label each. In the 2″ at the bottom of the board, mount five 1″ squares to designate the starting points for the players.

Also in the margins, you may want to label the sides of the playing area as North, South, East, and West.

Mount some red dots (made from a hole punch) in the center of about 20 of the 1″ squares at various places on the gray game area.

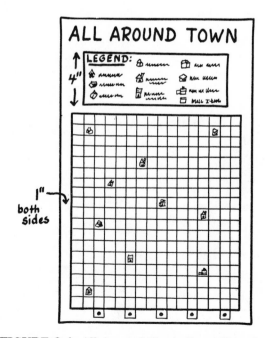

FIGURE 9-4: All Around Town Game Board

How to make the cards:

There are only ten game cards for the game. On ten 2″ by 3″ cards, mount the third set of buildings. Check to see that each of these cards has the building and its name as it appears on the legend.

How to make the dice:

Paint both of the cubes. On the sides of one of the cubes, write the numbers 1, 2, 3, 1, 2, 3. On the sides of the second cube write each of the following directions: North, South, East, West, Skip a Turn, and Any Direction. Then shellac the cubes for protection.

How to play the game:

The object of the game is to travel around town and collect a card from each of the places in the town. Since there are only ten cards, one for each place, the first player to land on that building gets that card.

Each player starts at one of the starting positions. In turn, the players roll both dice and move the number of spaces in the direction rolled. When a player lands directly on a building, then he may collect the card for that "place." If a player cannot move in the direction shown on his cubes, he loses his turn. If any player lands on a space with a red dot, that player may take another turn.

The game continues until all of the cards are collected. The player with the most cards wins the game.

Cross Country

The emphasis in this game is on the United States and the capitals. Through continuous use of the game, the children may even learn some interesting facts about each of the states, as well as its shape and location within the U.S.

Materials needed:

40″ by 30″ poster board (two 20″ by 30″ boards)
2 colors of construction paper
4 tokens
1 cube, numbered 1, 2, 3, 4, 5, 6.
paint

To make the game board:

On the poster board, draw the outline of the U.S., including Alaska and Hawaii. Paint each of the states, labeling the states, their capitals, and at least one large city for each of the larger states. In the four corners of the board draw a small airport. Using a ruler and a black marker, draw lines to connect the cities and the capitals. Each city should connect with only two or three other cities as shown in Figure 9-5. Each airport should connect with only two cities in its section of the map.

Making the game cards:

There are two sets of cards for this game. One set is the State Cards and the other set is the Travel Agent Cards.

Rule off one color of construction paper into fifty 3″ by 4″ sections to make the State Cards. On one side of each card draw the outline of a state so that you have one card for each state. Label the outlines with the states' abbreviations. On the opposite side of each of the cards, include the following information:

State's Name	Capital
Nickname of the State	State Bird
Date and Rank of Statehood	State Flower

To make the Travel Agent Cards, use another color of construction paper ruled off into 2″ by 3″ blocks. On these cards write directions such as the following:

Fly to Miami, Florida

Fly to Elko, Nevada.

Fly to the capital of Texas. You may collect the state card if nobody has it.

Fly to Billings, Montana.

Fly to Cedar Rapids, Iowa.

Fly to Salem, Oregon. Do NOT collect the state card.

Fly to the Northwestern Airport. Take another turn.

Fly to El Paso, Texas. Take another turn.

Fly to the capital of South Dakota. Do NOT collect the state card.

Fly to the capital of Arkansas. Do NOT collect the state card.

Fly to the Southeastern Airport. Take another turn.

Fly to the capital of Ohio. Do NOT collect the state card.

Fly to Los Angeles, California.

Collect one state card from the player on your right.

Fly to Burns, Oregon. Take another turn.

Fly to Tupelo, Mississippi. Take another turn.

Fly to the capital of Wisconsin.

Fly to Macon, Georgia.

Fly to Peoria, Illinois.

Fly to Honolulu, Hawaii. You may collect the state card if no one else has it.

Fly to Dodge City, Kansas. Take another turn.

Fly to the capital of Utah. Do NOT collect the state card.

Fly to Casper, Wyoming.

Fly to New York City, New York.

Fly to the capital of Washington. Do NOT collect the state card.

Fly to the capital of Maine. Do NOT collect the state card.

Fly to the capital of Michigan. Do NOT collect the state card.

Collect the TEXAS state card if no other player has it.

Change your position with that of the silver plane.

Collect one state card from one of the other players.

Ran out of gas; skip your next turn.

Fly ahead 1 city.

Fly ahead 3 cities.

Go back to your airport. Start again.

Stopping for dinner. Skip your next turn.

Stopping for the night. Skip your next turn.

Take another turn.

Good flying weather. Take another turn.

Change your position with that of the red plane.

Change your position with that of the green plane.

Change position of your plane with that of any other player.

Fly ahead 2 more cities.

Fly ahead 4 cities.

Give one of your state cards to the blue plane pilot.

Due to bad weather, skip your next turn.

EMERGENCY STOP! Give one of your state cards to the player on your left.

How to play the game:

The object of the game is to travel across the United States and collect the state cards as you visit the capitals of each state.

Each player starts from his own airport. The first player rolls the cube and moves along the airways. For example, if he rolls a 5, he would leave his airport and land 5 cities away. He may arrive at this city only by following the already prescribed airways, not by making a path of his own.

If the city he lands on happens to be a capital, he may then collect the state card for that state if no other player has it yet. If the city he lands on is *not* a capital, he may then visit the Travel Agent in that city by drawing a Travel Agent Card and following the directions.

Play continues until all of the state cards have been collected. The players must watch to see what cards are left towards the end of the game and plan to move in the directions of those states. The player with the most state cards at the end is the best Cross Country Traveler and is the winner.

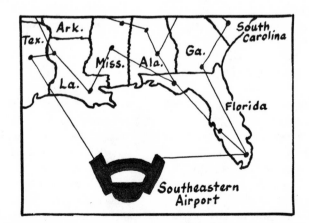

FIGURE 9-5: Section of Cross Country Game Board

10

Developing Study Units for the Health Shop

The Health Shop is designed to provide the children with an awareness of the complexity of the body and its many functions. This is achieved through studying the physical aspects of the body in the following units:

The Skin
The Skeleton
The Digestive System
The Respiratory System
The Muscular System
The Nervous System
The Circulatory System

Other units cover topics which emphasize the total well-being of each child and the importance of taking care of himself. Some units which deal with this aspect are:

Safety
First Aid
Nutrition

In this chapter we will explain the format for three sample units along with a Health Lab which deals with other topics for independent study and some enrichment activities.

UNITS

The format for all of the Health units is a packet which contains directions and activity sheets. The cover sheet for each packet lists all of the activities and provides a place where the children check off each activity as it is completed. It is a good idea to provide each set of partners with their own packet.

A sample cover sheet for the Safety Unit can look like the one shown in Figure 10-1.

Group:_____

Names:_____

SAFETY

▲ *1. Read* <u>*Safety Can Be*</u>
       <u>*Fun.*</u>
▲ *2. Filmstrip and poster.*
▲ *3. Emergency Phone Nos.*
▲ *4. Safety Skits*
▲ *5. Safety Quiz*

FIGURE 10-1: Sample Cover Sheet

SAFETY

The five activities for this unit as listed in Figure 10-1 will be explained in detail.

Activity 1: *Safety Can Be Fun*, by Munro Leaf

The teacher or member of the group reads half of the book *Safety Can Be Fun*, by Munro Leaf, to the rest of the group. Then each child contributes three safety "nit-wits" to be compiled into his group's book showing people breaking safety rules. Each page of the book is a colored picture of the "nit-wit" in action and two or three sentences describing it. After the group's book is finished, they read the rest of Munro Leaf's book to compare his "nit-wits" with theirs.

Activity 2: Filmstrip and Poster

Select a filmstrip dealing with some aspect of safety. After viewing the filmstrip, each set of partners thinks of a safety slogan and makes a poster illustrating it. Use various media for this project, such as construction paper, paint, chalk, yarn, and printed materials from newspapers and magazines.

Activity 3: Emergency Phone Numbers

It is important for every household to have certain phone numbers available for use in case of emergency. This project is an attractive way of displaying these numbers. (See Figure 10-2.)

Fold a 4½"×12" piece of colored construction paper into four equal sections. Glue the two ends together, forming a triangle.

On a 4"×2½" rectangle of another color of construction paper write the following:

Fire: _____

Police: _____

Doctor: _____

Hospital: _____

Neighbor: _____

The children find these phone numbers at home and record them in their proper places. Glue the phone numbers to the one side of the triangle. Decorate.

FIGURE 10-2: Emergency Phone Numbers

Activity 4: Safety Skits

Working in partners, the children choose a safety rule and perform a short skit about it. In the skit they should show the rule being broken and what might happen as a result. Use costumes and props to make the scene more dramatic.

Activity 5: Safety Quiz

The culminating activity of this unit is a safety quiz of multiple choice questions. Some sample questions that could be used in the quiz are given here:

1. The best place to fly a kite is:
   A.   in the woods.
   B.   in an open field.
   C.   in the street.
   D.   between buildings.

2 When you spill something on the floor:
   A.   wait until your mother cleans it up.
   B.   write a note telling everyone about it.
   C.   wipe it up right away.
   D.   put a rug over it.

3. To reach something on a high shelf:
   A.   stack books on a chair and then climb up.
   B.   always use a broom to knock it down.
   C.   put your little brother on your shoulders.
   D.   have someone taller get it for you.

4. When you use the bathtub:
   A.   always make sure the water isn't too hot before you get in.
   B.   leave the soap on the bottom of the tub.
   C.   practice the exercises you learned in gym.
   D.   take the radio in with you.

5. When a ball rolls into the street:
   A.   run right after it and catch it before it stops rolling.
   B.   send your little brother after it.
   C.   try to move it by throwing another ball.
   D.   stop and look both ways before going after it.

SKIN

The cover sheet for this unit packet would include these activities:
Vocabulary
Fingerprints
Fingerprint Art
Hair Under Microscope
Sensitivity Experiment
Drawing of the Skin
Filmstrip and Questions

Activity 1: Vocabulary

Using a dictionary and available resource books focusing on the skin, find the definitions for terms such as these:

follicle	epidermis
sweat	scab
pores	cell
dermis	gland

Activity 2: Fingerprints

Using a magnifying glass, each child examines his fingertips, noticing the various ridges and lines. The children then make prints of their fingertips by rolling each finger on an ink pad and then on a piece of practice paper. Before putting the prints on the good paper in the packet, make sure the practice prints are distinct, showing the lines of the skin clearly. The set of prints in the packet should be labeled with the children's names.

Activity 3: Fingerprint Art

Using finger paint, each child makes a picture on construction paper. The picture should consist entirely of clear fingerprints pressed down one at a time. Make sure the fingerprints are not smeared. For best results rub a small amount of finger paint on the fingertip.

Activity 4: Hair Under Microscope

Working in partners the children examine a single strand of hair under the microscope, being sure that the hair is extracted directly from the scalp. Compare both ends of the hair. Draw a diagram of both ends of the hair and label each.

Activity 5: Sensitivity Experiment

The Sensitivity Experiment is an activity with the purpose of answering three questions:

Does your skin have feeling?
Does your hair have feeling?
Do your fingernails have feeling?

The children work in partners for this activity. One person is blind-folded. The other child tries to touch the blindfolded person so gently that he can't feel anything. Touch him first with a cotton ball on his cheek, wrist, ear, and elbow. The blindfolded person should respond when he feels anything. Try touching him with a piece of paper on the same areas of his body. He should now be able to answer the first question: Does your skin have feeling?

Next, with a piece of paper very gently touch the blindfolded person's hair and fingernails. Then answer the other two questions.

The two children may reverse positions to make sure they are in agreement as to the answers to the three questions.

Activity 6: Drawing of the Skin

This sheet in the packet has a cross-section drawing of the skin with arrows pointing to eight parts of the skin. Below the drawing list the parts:

hair	follicle
sweat gland	dermis
blood vessel	epidermis
sweat pore	oil gland

In the blanks next to the arrows in the drawing, the children, using their resource books, label the parts of the skin.

Activity 7: Filmstrip and Questions

If available, show and discuss a filmstrip on the skin. Prepare questions that can be answered from the filmstrip or found in the resource books. Some sample questions may be:

1. What substance keeps the hair on your body soft and shiny?
2. What protects the tips of your fingers and toes?
3. What do the ridges on your fingertips tell you?
4. What does a scab do?
5. What does your skin do when you are cold?
6. How many layers of skin are there?
7. Do any two people have the same fingerprints?

SKELETON

This unit is comprised of six activities, which are:

Body Outline with Skeleton	Vocabulary
Filmstrip and Questions	Clay bones
Calcium Experiment	Drawing of the Skeleton

Activity 1: Body Outline

Cut off individual sections of large white butcher paper, large enough for one child's body outline. The student lies down on the paper as another student carefully traces around him. After the outline is traced, the child draws his skeleton inside his body using a health book, encyclopedia, or a posted diagram as a guide. After the body and bones are traced with crayon or magic marker, the bodies are cut out and displayed on the walls of the classroom.

Activity 2: Filmstrip and Questions

After viewing a filmstrip on the skeleton, the children can answer a set of teacher-prepared questions or make up a designated number of true-false or multiple choice questions. The questions the children prepared can then be exchanged and answered by the classmates.

Activity 3: Calcium Experiment

The materials needed for this experiment are vinegar, a chicken bone, and a jar.

Procedure: Completely submerge the chicken bone in a jar of vinegar for several days. Every three days take the bone out of the water and wipe off any film that has accumulated on it. When you do this, check to see if the bone bends. When the bone can be bent easily, wash it and then dry it. Try to break the bone. Does it break? The concept can then be explained.

Bones contain a lot of calcium. It is this calcium that makes the bone hard. In this experiment you removed the calcium by putting it into vinegar which is a mild acid. What happened to the bone?

Activity 4: Vocabulary

Prepare a list of vocabulary words to be matched with a list of their definitions. Some words you may use are:

joints	cranium	patella
marrow	clavicle	scapula
ligaments	sternum	sprain
calcium	vertebrae	fracture
cartilage		

Activity 5: Clay Bones

Each child selects at least two bones that he wants to shape out of clay.

After the bones are shaped, the child makes an accompanying name tag telling the name of the bone and where it is found in the body.

Activity 6: Drawing of the Skeleton

On the sheet in the packet with the diagram of a skeleton, label the following bones:

foot bones	femur	hand bones
ankle	vertebrae	cranium
fibula	ulna	scapula
humerus	pelvis	tibia
knee cap	wrist	ribs
radius	sternum	clavicle

HEALTH LAB

In addition to the Health units, a Health Lab is available for independent research and discovery. The lab can be utilized between units of study as well as when assigned unit activities are completed.

The four stations in the Health Lab are:

Station 1: Health Questions
Station 2: Micro-Units
Station 3: Health in the News
Station 4: Health Games

Station 1: Health Questions

Station 1 consists of health questions commonly asked by children. These questions are written on flashcards and numbered. Some sample questions are:

1. Why do we need a tongue?
2. How does sweat come out of our skin?
3. Why do we have bones?
4. What are bones made of?
5. Why do we blink our eyes?
6. What makes a bruise black and blue?
7. What is a scab?
8. How much blood do we have in our bodies?
9. What is a sprain?
10. Why are some people left-handed?
11. What makes people sneeze?

12. What is hay fever?
13. Why do people have different colors of skin?
14. What is a calorie?
15. What happens when my heart beats?

The child chooses one of the questions and using reference materials researches his answer. The questions and answers can be accumulated and kept in a booklet the child makes, entitled "All About Me."

Station 2: Micro-Units

Micro-units provide an avenue of in-depth study of various aspects of health. For this station the children can work by themselves or in partners. The child chooses a folder that deals with a health topic that he wants to pursue. The outside of each folder lists all the required activities for the completion of the folder. Inside the folder are the detailed directions and the necessary activity sheets.

A few micro-units that can be used are:

The Ear
The Eye
The Teeth

The Ear

The following is written on the outside of the folder:

To complete this folder do the following five activities:
1. World of Sound.
2. Read "How We Hear."
3. Questions.
4. Label drawing of the ear.
5. Research.

Materials found inside the folder:
World of Sound. Write a paragraph for each of the following:

1. Close your eyes for one minute. Listen carefully. Now write down all the different sounds you heard.
2. What kinds of sounds would you expect to hear in a forest?
3. What kinds of sounds would you expect to hear at the ocean?
4. What kinds of sounds would you expect to hear in a large, busy city?

How We Hear. The children read a prepared sheet with the diagram of the ear and the steps involved in hearing.

Questions. The children answer a set of prepared questions pertaining to the ear. For example:

1. What are the two purposes of the ear?
2. What are the three main parts of the ear?
3. Can a baby hear as soon as he is born?
4. What is a punctured eardrum?

Drawing of the Ear. Label the important parts of the ear.

Research. The children choose one of the following topics and prepare a report. They must include a picture, article, chart, slide, or transparency.

1. Sign Language
2. Lip Reading
3. Helen Keller
4. Hearing Aids
5. Deafness

The Eye

The following is written on the outside of the folder:

To complete this folder do the following three activities:
    1. Questions
    2. World of Sight
    3. Research

Materials found inside the folder:

Questions. The children answer a set of questions about the eye. For example:

What does it mean when someone has 20/20 vision?
What determines the color of your eyes?
What are three purposes of the eyelid?
What do eyelashes do?
What is farsightedness?
What is nearsightedness?

World of Sight. Choose one of the following:

1. Scrapbook.

    Using magazine pictures make a scrapbook called "The World Through My Eyes."

2. Interviews.

    Select ten people, five students and five adults, and record their answers to these questions:

What is the most beautiful thing you ever saw?

What would you miss seeing most if you lost your sight?

3. Drawing of the Eye.

Draw a diagram of the eye and label the following parts:

pupil	optic nerve
cornea	sclera
iris	retina
vitreos humor	

4. How We See.

Explain how the eye works like a camera. Use illustrations.

Research. Choose one of the following topics to research:

1. Color-Blindness
2. Diseases of the Eye
3. Contact Lenses
4. Eyes of Animals
5. Glasses

The report must include at least one of these visual aids—picture, transparency, slide, article from a newspaper or magazine, or diagram.

The Teeth

The following is written on the outside of the folder:

To complete this folder do the following five activities:
1. Good Dental Habits
2. Questions
3. Scrapbook
4. Research
5. Drawing of the tooth

Materials found inside the folder:

Good Dental Habits. Provide a pamphlet of an article for the children to read pertaining to good dental habits. The American Dental Association can provide you with such materials.

Questions. The students answer questions about the teeth such as:

What two sets of teeth does man have in his life?

What food contributes most to tooth decay?

What is the chief use of our teeth?

What is the commonest disease of man?

What element sometimes found in drinking water prevents tooth decay?

Scrapbook. Make a scrapbook showing the kinds of food that produce healthy teeth.

Research. Choose one of the following topics to explore:

1. The Four Kinds of Teeth
2. How Teeth Decay
3. Diseases of the Teeth

    Pyorrhea
    Gingivitis
    Trench Mouth

4. Dentistry

Drawing of the Tooth. Label the following parts of the tooth:

root	cementum	dentin
crown	enamel	pulp

Station 3: Health in the News

This station offers interesting and up-to-date information on health and some of the current trends and findings in health. The children can contribute to this by making folders of health articles and pictures they bring in and putting them on file in the "Health in the News" box. They absorb much information by just browsing through the folders.

Station 4: Health Games

The fourth station gives the children a variety of health games to play. Some of the games are:

Missing Bones—skeletal system
Health Hazard—safety
Heart Beat—heart and circulatory system
Sorting Senses—five senses
X-Ray—organs of the body

Missing Bones

Materials needed:

—20"×20" poster board
—4 tokens, each a different color
—1 cube numbered 0, 1, 2, 3, 4, 5
—ditto with a 10" drawing of a skeleton on it
—construction paper

Making the puzzle pieces:

Using the skeleton master, run off one skeleton on five different colors of construction paper. Four of these skeletons can be mounted on stiff cardboard and then laminated. Cut each skeleton into at least 12 puzzle pieces. Store each skeleton puzzle in separate envelopes.

Making the game board:

In the center of the board mount the fifth skeleton construction paper diagram. Label some of the important bones on this skeleton.

Cut approximately twenty 3″ footprints from gray construction paper. Mount two footprints in the bottom right-hand corner of the board, indicating the starting point. The other 18 are mounted in a path around the skeleton. On each of the 18 footprints write directions or incomplete sentences similar to the following:

—Bend your knee cap.
—Another name for the vertebrae is _____ .
—Scratch your skull.
—Move your humerus up and down.
—Point to your neighbor's collarbone.
—Add a puzzle piece (written on about 5 footprints).
—The _____ is the biggest leg bone.

In an open space around the game board write the name of the game.

Playing the Game:

Each player starts out with an envelope of his own skeletal puzzle. The object of the game is to be the first player to put the puzzle together. All the players start on the starting footprints. The first player rolls the cube, moves the designated number of spaces, and follows the direction on the footprint. Play continues around the board until a player puts all his puzzle pieces together. This requires the players to go around the board three or four times. The player who has put his puzzle together and has found the "missing bones" is declared the winner.

Health Hazard

Materials needed:

—15″×20″ poster board
—construction paper
—1 wooden cube numbered 0, 1, 2, 3, 4, 5
—8 tokens painted four colors (two of each)

Making the game board:

On a 12"×12" square of construction paper rule off 1" blocks with a magic marker. Darken in the four corner squares. Mount this on the poster board. Next to the 12"×12" construction paper outline two 3½"×6" rectangles to designate the placement of the playing cards. Arrange the name of the game, "Health Hazard," in an attractive manner on the board.

Making the playing cards:

Rule off 3½"×6" rectangles on construction paper. In each section write a multiple choice type question exhibiting a safety rule. For example:

The best place to swim is:
- (a) at a lonely beach.
- (b) in the middle of the ocean.
- (c) at a pool after closing time.
- (d) at a beach or pool where there is a lifeguard.

When walking at night:
- (a) wear light-colored clothing.
- (b) walk in the direction of the traffic.
- (c) wear dark-colored clothing.
- (d) walk side-by-side with your friends on the road.

Playing the game:

Each player places his two tokens on one of the squares on his side of the 12"×12" construction paper. The cards are placed face down in one of the rectangles on the board. The object of the game is to get both of your tokens to the opposite edge of the checkerboard.

The first player chooses a card and reads it aloud. He tells his choice for the correct answer. If all the players agree with him he rolls the cube and moves that number of spaces. He is permitted to move one token that number of spaces or a combination of both his tokens that number of spaces. If his answer is incorrect he is not allowed to roll the cube. Play continues in this fashion until a player gets both tokens to the opposite side of the checkerboard. During the game if a player lands on a space already occupied by another player he can bump that token back to its starting position.

Heart Beat

Materials needed:

—15"×20" poster board
—construction paper

—4 tokens, each a different color
—1 wooden cube numbered 1, 2, 3, 1, 2, 3

Making the game board:

The game board is set up vertically. Cut a 12"-long piece of construction paper, 2" wide. Divide it into 1" rungs like a ladder. Mount this on the right-hand side of the board, placing at the bottom of the strip a circle labeled "Start." At the top of the ladder place a drawing of the heart, indicating the winner's point. On the left-hand side of the board, make a drawing of a large heart and write the title of the game.

Making the playing cards:

Rule of 3½"×5½" rectangles on construction paper. Write approximately 30 multiple choice questions that deal with parts of the heart, how the heart works, heart diseases, etc. For example:

The largest chambers of the heart are:
  (1) atrium
  (2) ventricle
  (3) aorta

Blood from the body flows into the heart through:
  (1) veins
  (2) arteries
  (3) valves

A man's heart normally beats about:
  (1) 120 times a minute
  (2) 50 times a minute
  (3) 70 times a minute

It would be convenient to have the questions and answers in a Heart Beat Answer Booklet for the children to check each other.

Playing the game:

Place the cards face down on the large drawing of the heart. The players place their tokens on the circle at the bottom of the ladder. The first player draws a heart question and reads it aloud. He then reads the question again, filling in the correct ending. Another player looks up the answer in the answer booklet to see if he is correct. If the correct answer is given, the player rolls the cube and moves that number of spaces up the ladder. When an incorrect answer is given he is not allowed to roll the cube. When each player is finished with a card, he places it on the bottom of the pile. The player who reaches the heart at the top of the ladder first is the winner.

Sorting Senses

Materials needed:

—15″×20″ poster board
—construction paper
—1 wooden cube numbered 0, 1, 2, 3, 4, 5

Making the game board:

Cut thirty 1½″ squares of any color construction paper. Arrange these squares in a path, using the top 2/3 of the poster board. Label the starting square and the finishing square. On the lower 1/3 of the board, outline five 1½″×2½″ rectangles. In each of the rectangles write one of the five senses; see, hear, taste, smell, and feel. Above each rectangle, mount a small drawing to illustrate each sense. For example:

> sight—moon
> smell—flower
> hearing—bell
> taste—apple
> feeling—hypodermic needle

Rule off one more 1½″×2½″ rectangle to designate the placement of the playing cards.

Making the playing cards:

On 1½″×2½″ rectangles of construction paper write approximately ten words or phrases to exemplify each of the senses. For example:

sight—fog
    lightning
    sunset
smell—flower
    air pollution
    spoiled food
hearing—howling wind
    laughter

    music
taste—cough medicine
    salty
    sour
feeling—bee sting
    sprained ankle
    fluffy pillow

Try to choose words or phrases which clearly show a dominating sense over the others.

Playing the game:

Place the cards face down on the unlabeled rectangle. Players place their tokens on the starting square. The first player chooses a card and reads it aloud, and then places it on the sense that it best represents. If all the players agree, he rolls the cube and moves that number of spaces. If he does not choose the most characteristic sense, he is not permitted to roll the cube. The player to reach the finish first wins.

X-Ray

Materials needed:

—20"×30" poster board
—construction paper
—transparencies
—4 tokens painted different colors
—1 wooden cube numbered 1, 2, 3, 4, 5, 6

Making the game board:

Cut five 5"×7" rectangles, each of a different color of construction paper. Write on each one of the rectangles one of the following:

> 1—Skeletal System
> 2—Digestive System
> 3—Nervous System
> 4—Circulatory System
> 5—Respiratory System

Mount these five rectangles in a row across the bottom of the game board.

Mount a 4½"×12" rectangle in the center at the top of the board. Label this rectangle the X-Ray Lab. Place five entrance doors around the Lab. Make hallways leading from the five doors at the X-Ray Lab to the five rectangles at the bottom of the board as shown in Figure 10-3.

Making the transparency cards:

Divide tracing paper, 8½"×10½", into four 4¼"×5¼" rectangles. For each system, trace drawings of the parts of the system in the rectangles. Draw an arrow to the part of the system you want the child to name and label that arrow with a number. For example, the digestive system would have two basic drawings—one of the head showing the following parts: tongue, salivary glands, epiglottis, larynx, esophagus, mouth; and one from the throat to the bladder showing the following: esophagus, stomach, intestines, liver, pancreas, kidneys, bladder. The skeletal system would have one basic drawing, which might show some of the following parts: skull, vertebrae, clavicle, scapula, sternum, ribs, humerus, pelvic bone, ulna, radius, femur, fibula, tibia.

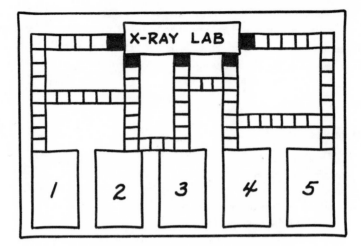

FIGURE 10-3: X-Ray Game Board

You will have a different number of transparencies for each system, depending on the parts you want the child to recognize. Mount the transparencies on the colored construction paper that represents each system on the game board. Make an answer booklet so the children can receive immediate feedback as to the right answers.

Playing the game:

The players place their tokens in the X-Ray Lab. Place each set of transparencies on the proper system. The object of the game is to get one X-ray (transparency) from each system and to be the first player to return to the Lab to develop them. The players roll the cube and move that number of spaces. As soon as the player reaches a system he draws an X-ray transparency and tells the name of the part the arrow indicates. The player on his left looks up his answer in the answer booklet and tells him if he is correct or not. If the right answer is given he keeps the X-ray. If he is incorrect he puts the X-ray at the bottom of the pile. Play continues with each player trying to get one X-ray transparency from each system. When he does this, he heads back to the X-Ray Lab. The first player there wins.

11

Expressing Yourself Correctly in the Language Shop

Grammar is not an outmoded area of study. We emphasize the use of good grammar through units, self-practice activities, and games. Learning the basic parts of speech, punctuation, capitalization, etc., can be made interesting when presented and reinforced in unusual ways, such as through games.

This chapter will present a sample Poetry Unit, self-quizzes, some card games, and a number of board games.

PRELIMINARY ACTIVITIES

One of the activities that can be incorporated in this shop at the beginning of the year is a series of tapes and accompanying worksheets reinforcing language skills. The taped lessons explain the skill and give directions for the worksheet.

Activities that can be used at any time throughout the year are the language self-quizzes. (See Figure 11-1.)

These self-quizzes can be designed for practice in many language skills. Some examples are:

> noun markers
> plurals
> possessives
> abbreviations
> capitals
> verb tenses

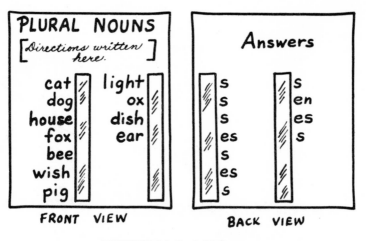

FIGURE 11-1: Self Quizzes

POETRY UNIT (POETRY SLIDE PROGRAM)

Poetry can open the door to a child's inner expression. With just a few selected words a child can create an image manifesting his thoughts, which no one can say are right or wrong.

Beginning poets need a stimulus to spark their enthusiasm for poetic writing. Pictures serve this purpose very well.

It is easier for the beginning poets to follow a specific form of poetry. We have used the following styles:

1. *Haiku*—This style consists of three lines. The first line has five syllables, the second line has seven, and the third line has five.

2. *Cinquaine*—This pattern consists of five lines. The first has one word which tells what the poem is about. The second line has two words, the third line has three, the fourth line has four, and the last line has one.

3. *Limerick*—Limericks are nonsense poems. They have five lines. The first, second, and fifth lines rhyme, and the third and fourth lines rhyme.

To retain the enthusiasm for poetry, the beginning unit should culminate in a big production displaying the children's poetic talents. A slide presentation is an ideal way of doing this.

Before any writing takes place, the child selects a picture that captures his interest. He chooses the style of poetry he wants to use and composes his poem. The child then mounts his picture on construction paper and writes his poem underneath.

Using a visual maker, make a slide of each child's picture. Arrange all the slides according to subject matter and have each child record his poem on tape to correspond with the sequence of slides. A nice added touch is to tape background music on another tape. This can be played simultaneously with the tape of poems to enhance the mood.

Another way of displaying poems the children write is through a "Poetry Pamphlet." Instead of finding a picture to write about, the children are given a topic or a choice of topics. They write their poems and draw practice pictures illustrating them. Then each child is given a regular ditto master and a colored ditto master of his choice. He reproduces his poem and picture on the ditto, using the colored one as he desires. Run off as many as necessary to enable each child to have a copy of all the poems to make up his pamphlet.

— — — — — — —

The remainder of this chapter will be devoted to explaining the board and card games that reinforce all the language skills.

CARD GAMES

Sparts

Materials needed:

—construction paper

Making the cards:

Rule off the construction paper into 52 3"×4" sections. On each card write one of the following:

Nouns		*Verbs*	
bus	letter	clean	write
book	candy	sing	walking
pencil	card	talk	standing
snake	child	drive	throw
chair	cat	run	saw
crayon	apple	looking	kicked
school		playing	

Adjectives		*Pronouns*	
tall	green	it	our
long	short	we	mine
shiny	nice	you	your
new	large	his	he
old	dirty	her	she
pretty	round	them	they
small		us	

Playing the game:

This game deals with the four parts of speech: nouns, verbs, adjectives, and pronouns. The players must be able to distinguish these four parts of speech that make up the four suits in the game.

The rules of the game are as follows:

1. Dealer shuffles and deals all the cards.
2. The first player puts one of his cards face up in the center of the playing area. He should play his high cards first. (The cards are numbered like a regular deck.)
3. Playing in a clockwise direction, each player puts down a card of the same suit (part of speech) as the one played first. The player whose card has the highest number on it takes all four cards. If a player does not have a card to follow that part of speech, he must play any card of another suit. He cannot take the four cards when he does this, even if his card is higher than the other three.
4. The player who takes the four cards must play the first card of the next round.
5. Play continues until all the cards have been played.
6. At the end of play each player counts the number of cards he has collected, and that is his score. The first player to reach 50 is the winner.

Contraction Search ✓

Materials needed:

—construction paper

Making the cards:

Rule off the construction paper into 52 3"×4" sections. In each section write one of the following:

isn't	is not	haven't	have not
aren't	are not	she's	she is
didn't	did not	they're	they are
wasn't	was not	we'd	we would
weren't	were not	they've	they have
couldn't	could not	I'm	I am
wouldn't	would not	I'll	I will
shouldn't	should not	I've	I have
can't	can not	I'd	I would
won't	will not	you'll	you will
you're	you are	they'll	they will

| he's | he is | she'd | she would |
| hasn't | has not | doesn't | does not |

Playing the game:

The object of Contraction Search is to match the contraction to the two words it stands for. This game can be played with 2-6 players.

Deal eight cards to each player. The remaining cards are placed in the center face down with one card face up designating the discard pile.

The first player draws a card and tries to make as many matches as possible. All his matches are placed face up in front of him. He must discard a card from his hand at every turn.

Play continues in this manner until a player runs out of cards and is then declared the winner. (He must have the most contraction matches in front of him.)

Noun Nuisance

Materials needed:

—construction paper

Making the cards:

Rule off the construction paper into 52   2½"×4" sections. Write 26 common nouns and 26 proper nouns on the cards.

Playing the game:

This game is similar to the game of War. It is for two players. All the cards are dealt out and placed face down in a pile in front of each player. At the same time both players take their top cards from their piles and place them face up in the center of the playing area. The player whose card is the proper noun wins the pair. (The proper nouns are not capitalized on the cards.) If both cards are proper nouns or common nouns they remain face up in the center. Players take their next top cards and place them in the center. If there is a proper noun in this set that player wins all the cards. The first player to accumulate all the cards or the player with the most cards at the end of a designated time is the winner.

BOARD GAMES

Bicycle Park Race

Materials needed:

—20"×30" poster board

—construction paper

—1 wooden cube

—4 1"-long dowel rod pieces painted different colors to be used as tokens

Making the cards:

Rule off 4½"×2" sections of the construction paper. Have available a list of abbreviations and the corresponding words they stand for. On half of the cards write the abbreviations and on the other half write the words that they stand for.

Making the game board:

Using construction paper and Magic Markers, make a winding path on the poster board (Figure 11-2). At regular intervals along the park path place the following pictures with the accompanying directional phrases written in the block next to it:

Picture	*Directions*
Apple tree	Pick some apples.
Park bench	Take a rest break.
Ice cream peddler	Take an ice cream break.
Rock	Take a rock-sitting break.
Swing	Take a swing break.
Weeds	Pick some weeds.
Lake and sailboat	Take a boat ride.
Park bench	Take a rest break.
Apple tree	Pick some apples.
Daisies	Pick some flowers.
Bike rack	WINNER
(at the end)	

Making the cube:

Paint the entire cube. Then write the numbers 4, 5, 6, 4, 5, and 6 on small pieces of construction paper, glue on the sides of the cube, and shellac.

Playing the game:

The object of the game is to match the abbreviations with their corresponding words. The dealer deals six cards to each player; the rest of the cards are placed face down. The first player draws a card and checks his cards to see if he can make any matches. If he can, he places the match in front of him face up and rolls the numbered cube to see how many spaces he moves on the park path. If he does not make a match, he does not move, and the next

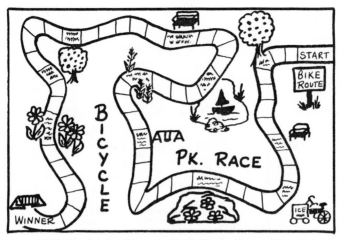

FIGURE 11-2: Bicycle Park Race Game Board

player plays. If a player lands on a directional phrase block, he misses his turn. Play continues until the first player reaches the bike rack, and is the winner.

Sentence Climber

Materials needed:

—20″×30″ poster board
—construction paper
—2 1″-cubes
—4 1″-long sections of dowel rod painted different colors to be used as tokens.

Making the cards:

Rule off eighty 3″×4″ blocks of construction paper. Write the word "Noun" on twenty of the cards; write "Verb" on another 20 cards. On ten cards write "Why," on another ten write "Where," on another ten cards write "How," and on the last ten write "When."

Making the cubes:

Paint each cube a different color. On one cube write the numbers 1, 2, and 3, and on the second cube write the numbers 4, 5, and 6.

Making the board:

Make four ladders, each 5″ wide and 21″ high, with the steps 1″ apart. Under the bottom step of each ladder write the word "Start." Label the ladders at the top—1, 2, 3, and 4. Place five ½" strips, 22" long, between each ladder. At the top of the board write the title "Sentence Climber." (See Figure 11-3.)

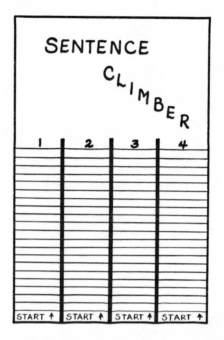

FIGURE 11-3: Sentence Climber Game Board

Playing the game:

The object of the game is to create a sentence using a "noun" card, a "verb" card, and one or more of the question cards.

The dealer deals eight cards to each player, the rest of the cards face down, with one card face up to start a discard pile. The first player looks at his cards and tries to create a sentence, using as many of his cards as he can that will fit to make a complete sentence. He must include at least one noun card, one verb card, and one of any of the other four cards. If his sentence is made up of three or four cards, he rolls the 1, 2, 3 cube to see how many spaces he moves up his ladder. If his sentence is made up of five or more cards, he rolls the 4, 5, 6 cube to see how many spaces he moves up his ladder. He places the used cards in front of him, and at his next turn draws that number of cards from the pile. He will have eight cards in his hand at all times. The player to reach the top of his ladder first is the winner.

Short Stop

Materials needed:

—construction paper
—20"×15" poster board
—4 wooden cubes
—4 1"-section dowel rods painted different colors to be used as tokens

Making the game board:

In the middle of the poster board make a baseball diamond labeling home, first, second, and third bases. Label locker rooms, dugouts, and the outfield as shown in Figure 11-4.

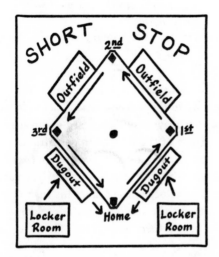

FIGURE 11-4: Short Stop Game Board

Making the cubes:

On each side of the four painted cubes attach a piece of construction paper ¾" square, writing noun substitutes as follows:

I	he	them
my	her	his
yours	she	theirs
ours	your	you
they	its	mine

it	him	hers
our	we	me
us	their	it

Shellac all the cubes in order to protect them.

Making the cards:

On 3"×4" sections of construction paper write sentences pertaining to baseball that require one of the noun substitutes. Some examples as they would appear on the cards are:

The ball flew to the shortstop.
Jill and I both struck out.
Doug is the captain of the team.
Sue asked, "Who wants to be scorekeeper with *Sue?*"
Jason said, "This bat is *Jason's.*"
All the runs made in the seventh inning were *Jill's, Sue's, and mine.*

Playing the game:

The object of the game is to roll a noun substitute that fits your card. All the tokens are placed in the locker rooms. The cards are placed face down in the outfield. The first player chooses a card and reads his sentence aloud. He rolls the cubes. If one of the four noun substitutes showing can replace the noun underlined on his card, he moves his token to the dugout. If he does not roll such a noun substitute he may not move. The card is then placed in the other outfield pile. The next player takes his turn. The pattern of play is from the locker room, to the dugout, batter's plate at home, first base, second base, third base, and then home plate. The first player to reach home wins.

When the pile is depleted, the cards are reshuffled and the players continue playing.

Fort Hero

Materials needed:

—20"×30" poster board
—colored construction paper
—1 wooden cube
—4 tokens, or 2 Indian tokens and 2 cowboy tokens

Making the cube:

On each side of a painted cube write the numbers 1, 2, 3, 4, 5, and 6. Shellac the cube.

Making the game board:

Cut brown construction paper, 1¼ " wide, into strips of the following lengths:

    2—25" strips
    2—12½" strips
    2—9" strips
    2—14" strips
    4—2½" strips

Place these strips according to the illustration shown in Figure 11-5, marking 1¼" sections on each.

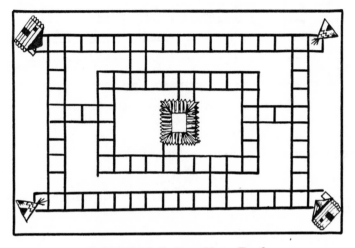

FIGURE 11-5: Fort Hero Trails

Cut six 1¼"-squares of brown construction paper, to be used as starting points in each of the four corners. The extra two are used to connect the inner rectangle to the fort.

Using two colors of construction paper, cut 14 1¼"-squares of each. These squares are mounted at random intervals on the brown squares of the trail. On each of these colored squares place an asterisk or some other distinguishing mark.

At two opposite corners of the trail make two teepees. At the other two corners make log cabins.

Between the two starting points at one end of the board, mount two 2½"×3½" pieces of construction paper the same color as one of the squares denoted by the asterisk. At the other end of the board place two 2½"×3½" pieces of construction paper matching the other color. At one end label the mounted cards "Predicate Cards" and "Predicate Discard Pile." The cards at the other end are labeled "Subject Cards" and "Subject Discard Pile."

In the center of the board mount a $4'' \times 4\frac{1}{2}''$ fort. The completed board will look like Figure 11-6.

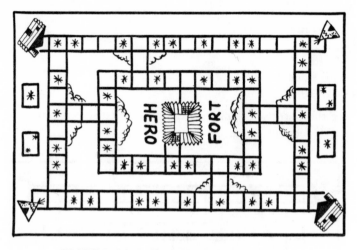

FIGURE 11-6: Fort Hero Game Board

Making the playing cards:

You will need two colors of construction paper, one color for the subject cards and one color for the predicate cards. On the $2'' \times 3''$ subject cards write subjects such as: the computer, the floor, my friends and I, and the little girl.

On $2'' \times 3''$ predicate cards write predicates such as: answered the telephone, is broken, is muddy, and went to sleep.

On the backs of these cards the asterisk or other distinguishing mark that you used can be written.

Playing the Game:

The object of the game is to make five complete sentences before entering the fort. Each player places his token on either a teepee or a log cabin. The first player rolls the cube and moves his token accordingly. If he lands on a colored asterisk space, he draws the top card from that pile. In his subsequent turns he tries to land on a square of the other color. Once he has a card of each color in his hand, he must decide if he has a realistic sentence. If he does he places it face up on the table in front of him. If he doesn't, during his next turn he rolls the cube and moves toward an asterisk. When he lands on one, he discards that color from his hand and draws a new one. Play continues this way. Make sure the players roll the cube only once per turn and that they hold only two cards in their hands, one of each color. When the players have five sentences face up in front of them, their following turns are devoted to moving their tokens to the fort. The first one there wins.

Word Knowledge

Materials needed:

—construction paper
—1 painted cube
—20″×30″ poster board
—4 painted tokens
—4 dictionaries

Making the game board:

In the upper right hand corner of the board place a 3″ square of construction paper, labeled "Start." Cut many 1½″ squares of different colors of construction paper. Using these squares make a path around the board ending at the bottom left-hand corner, which is labeled "King of Words." Place one short-cut strip somewhere along the path. In four open sections of the board place 3″×3″ cards, one labeled A-E, one F-P, one Q-Z, and one the discard pile. Your game board should look similar to the one shown in Figure 11-7.

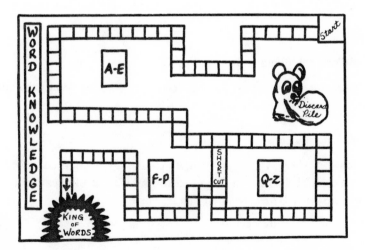

FIGURE 11-7: Word Knowledge Game Board

Making the cube and cards:

On the painted cube write the numbers 2, 3, 4, 5, 6, and 7. Shellac.

On 3″×3″ cards write words that can be found in the dictionary and the meanings you want the children to find. For example:

even   —meaning pertaining to numbers
coach   —meaning pertaining to carriages and horses
note   —meaning pertaining to music
moccasin—meaning pertaining to snakes
lace   —meaning pertaining to shoes
vessel   —meaning pertaining to transportation

Playing the game

Sort the cards into the correct squares on the board. The first player chooses a card from one of the piles and reads it. In order to roll the cube he must find his word in the dictionary and read the correct meaning that is indicated on the card. When he does this correctly he rolls the cube and moves that number of spaces towards the goal—"King of Words." All the used cards are placed in the discard pile. Each player takes his turn in the same way. The winner is the first one to reach "King of Words."

Downhill Racer

Materials needed:

—construction paper
—20″×30″ poster board
—2 tokens

Making the game board:

Construct a ski slope, plotting a course of nine flags down the hill, and finish the board as shown in Figure 11-8.

Making the cards:

On 2″×3″ cards write nouns that you want the children to be able to describe through association. Below each word write a number denoting how many words may be used to describe it. Some examples are:

octopus—5   glacier—8
pollution—7   potato—4

Playing the game:

This game is designed for play in partners. The object of the game is to guess the word your partner is describing to you. The first player draws a card. He then formulates a description of his word, using the number on his

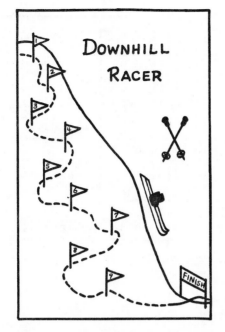

FIGURE 11-8: Downhill Racer Game Board

card. His partner has one chance to guess the word. If he guesses it correctly, the partners may move their token to the next flag down the slope. When his answer is incorrect, they do not move their token. The first team that reaches the finish line wins.

Publisher

Materials needed:
—20"×15" poster board
—construction paper
—4 tokens
—1 painted wooden cube

Making the game board:

Construct a road starting in the lower left-hand corner of the board and ending at the middle of the right-hand edge (see Figure 11-9). The blocks along the road are divided into 1¼" segments which are labeled by either a chapter, a "Proofread," or a letter symbol. In the upper right-hand corner label two 2½"×3½" rectangles: (1) Letters from your publisher. (2) Proofread your chapters. Just below the rectangles and at the end of the road mount a truck with the sign indicating the final goal: "On Its Way to the Bookstores!"

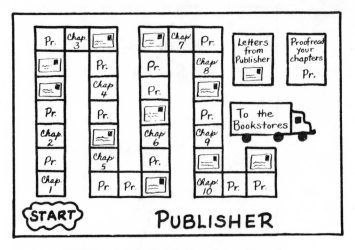

FIGURE 11-9: Publisher Game Board

Making the cards:

On one color of 2″×3″ construction paper cards write messages that could be found in the letters from your publisher. For example:

"Sorry, your last chapter got lost in the mail. Go back and rewrite it."

"Temporary set-back. Move back two spaces."

"Sorry, spilled mustard on your last chapter. Go back and continue from there."

"Good work; keep it up!"

"Fantastic work! Move ahead two spaces."

"Bad news. All your chapters were ruined by a flood in the office. Go back to start."

On the other color of cards write pairs of words, one of which *should* be capitalized but is not. For example:

> thursday—week
> people—tony
> highway—market lane
> spain—country
> miss—letter
> october—city

Make approximately 35 of these cards. For clarity, the colors of the cards should correspond with the symbols used on the game board.

Making the cube:

On the sides of the wooden cube paint these numbers: 1, 2, 3, 1, 2, 3.

Playing the game:

In the course of the game the players may land on one of three symbols. The safety zones are signified by the chapter symbols. The proofread symbols require the player to choose a "Proofread your chapter" card. The player must read the words on this card and tell which one needs a capital letter. The letter symbol calls for the player to choose a letter from the corresponding pile. He must follow the directions written on this card.

The players take their turns rolling the cube. The first player to complete his book by reaching the truck wins.

Railroad Game

Materials needed:

—20"×30" poster board
—construction paper
—4 tokens
—1 painted cube numbered 1, 2, 3, 4, 5, 6

Making the game board:

Two railroad stations are placed at opposite ends of the board (see Figure 11-10). Both the starting station and the ending station are labeled with names such as Wabash Station and Iron City Station. Then make a winding railroad track connecting the two stations. At irregular intervals on the track mount small brown circles. In two places around the track mount 3½"×2½" cards.

Making the cards:

On 3½"×2½" cards of construction paper write sentences deleting the verb, with a choice of two verbs given below the sentence. These missing verb sentences emphasize the usage of the correct form of the word. Some verbs that could be used are:

did—done
isn't—aren't
was—were
went—gone
saw—seen
don't—doesn't

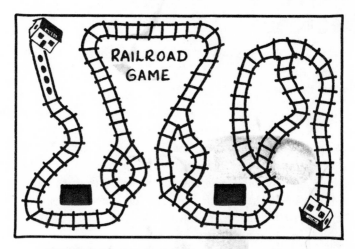

FIGURE 11-10: Railroad Game Game Board

Playing the game:

The object of the game is to be the first player to arrive at the ending station. The first player draws a card and reads the sentence, filling in the blank. If he fills in the blank with the correct form of the verb he rolls the cube and moves that number of spaces. If the player fills in the sentence incorrectly he does not move. When a player lands on a space on the track that has a small brown circle, he has been confronted with a cow on the track and he must skip his next turn. Play continues in the same manner until a player reaches the ending station and is declared the winner.

Desert Dialogue

Materials needed:

—20″×30″ poster board
—construction paper
—15 6″×9″ brown envelopes
—4 tokens
—1 painted cube numbered 1, 2, 3, 1, 2, 3

Making the game board:

Make a winding path starting at the bottom left-hand corner and ending at the upper right-hand corner (see Figure 11-11). At intervals along the path place a cave, cactus hill, snake pit, and a watering hole at the end. On the path segments, place at random rock symbols denoting the small rock in the center of the board, labeled, "What's under the rock?" On the section of the path next to Cactus Hill write, "Ouch!" Write "Hiss. . ." on the section of the path next to the snake pit.

Making the cards:

On 2″×3″ sections of brown construction paper write the following directions that are to be placed on the rock in the center of the board:

4—Sandstorm! Hide in the cave and skip a turn.
2—Go back two spaces.
2—Go back three spaces.
2—Move ahead two spaces.
2—Move ahead three spaces.
1—Saddlebag #1
1—Saddlebag #2
1—Saddlebag #3
1—Saddlebag #4
1—Saddlebag #5
1—Saddlebag #6
1—Saddlebag #7
1—Saddlebag #8
1—Saddlebag #9
1—Saddlebag #10
1—Saddlebag #11
1—Saddlebag #12
1—Saddlebag #13
1—Saddlebag #14

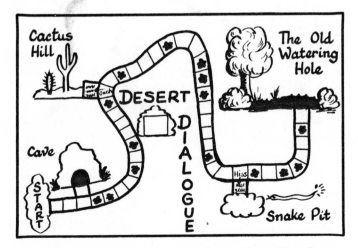

FIGURE 11-11: Desert Dialogue Game Board

On 2"-wide strips of construction paper write 14 sentences, some requiring quotation marks and some not. Each sentence should be on a different color of paper. The quotation marks are not included in the 14 sentences. For example:

I need a drink of water moaned Billy the Kid.

Jesse James said that the sun was too hot.

Jesse James said hope the watering hole isn't dry.

Billy the Kid said to Jesse we can sleep in the cave.

Next to each word write small numbers showing the sequence of the words in the sentence. Laminate the strips and cut the words apart. The size of these cards may vary according to the length of the word.

On four different colors of construction paper or oaktag cut four sets of quotation marks and commas one inch high. Also make four letter C's two inches high.

Making the envelopes:

Label 14 of the brown envelopes "Saddlebag #1" through "Saddlebag #14." On the fifteenth one write "Quotation Marks, Capitals, Commas." Put each sentence in one of the saddlebag envelopes. During the year's time you can change the sentences or keep putting them in different envelopes. The punctuation marks and the C's are stored in the envelope marked as such.

Playing the game:

Each player has in front of him a set of punctuation marks and a letter C. The first player rolls the cube and moves that number of spaces. If he lands on a rock he draws a card from the rock pile. If it is a direction card he follows the directions. If the card has a Saddlebag number on it, he takes the corresponding envelope and places the words of the sentence in the correct order in front of him. He reads the sentence aloud and then places any punctuation marks and the letter C over the letter of the word that needs to be capitalized. If the sentence needs no corrections he makes a statement to the rest of the players saying so. If the Saddlebag is done correctly, the player stays where he is on the trail. If it is incorrect, the player moves back two spaces. Any time a player lands on the "Ouch!" or "Hiss . . ." blocks he must skip a turn. Play continues until a player crosses the desert and reaches the watering hole.

Ask Me? Tell Me.

Materials needed:

—20"×30" poster board
—three colors of construction paper
—1 cube with sides painted the three colors
—4 tokens

Making the board:

This game board is divided into two parts. On one-half mount three 3"×6" cards, one of each color. Next to one card write "1 Point" and next to one of the other cards write "2 Points." On the other side of the board draw a circle approximately 11" in diameter. Construct a winding circular path within the circle ending in the center. The area left in the center should be about three inches in diameter. Make a star in this area denoting the winner. (See Figure 11-12.)

Making the cards:

Using the same color of construction paper as the colored rectangles labeled "1 Point" on the board, write sentences leaving out the end punctuation marks. For example:

Several squirrels ran up the tree
How many games do you have
The baseball game was rained out

Using the same color of construction paper as the colored rectangle labeled "2 Points," write directions that will require the players to make up either an asking sentence or a telling sentence. For example:

Asking sentence that begins with "which."
Asking sentence that begins with "how."
Tell me what you like to do.
Tell me what a park is.

On the third color of construction paper write direction cards such as:

Skip a turn.
Switch places with another player.
Go back to start.

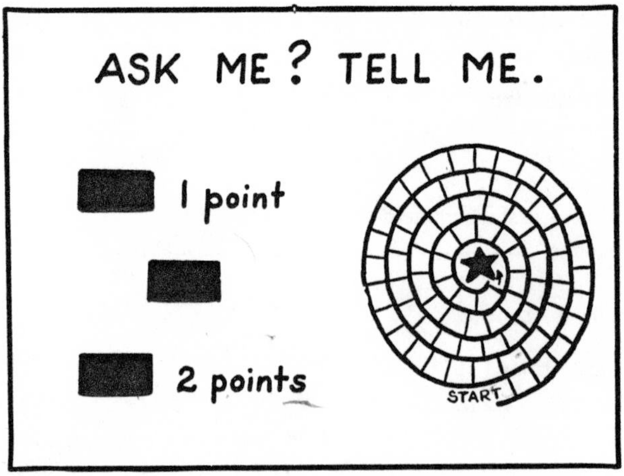

FIGURE 11-12: Ask Me? Tell Me.   Game Board

Move ahead 2 spaces.
Move back 2 spaces.

Playing the game:

The object of the game is to get to the winner's star first. The first player rolls the cube and draws a card of that color. When a 1-point card is drawn, he reads the sentence and then states whether a period or question mark is needed. When a 2-point card is drawn, he reads what kind of sentence he must make and then proceeds to do so. If the player does the chosen card correctly, he moves either the one or two spaces. When a player rolls the color signifying the direction cards, he draws one and follows the direction. Play continues in this fashion until a player reaches the winner's star.

Maze Craze

Materials needed:

—20"×30" poster board
—1 piece of 18"×24" construction paper
—4 painted tokens
—1 wooden cube numbered 1, 2, 3, 4, 5, 6

Making the board:

Mount the 18"×24" construction paper on the board, leaving a 4½"-margin at the top, 1½"-margin at the bottom, and 1"-margins at the sides.

Rule off the construction paper into 1″ squares with a light Magic Marker. Find the center four blocks and mount four 1″ squares of construction paper, each of a different color to correspond with the four tokens. Cut four 1½″ squares to match the tokens and mount as shown in Figure 11-13.

With black Magic Marker outline some of the segments on the construction paper to represent a maze.

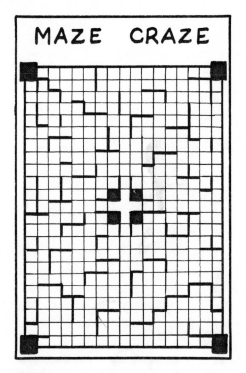

FIGURE 11-13: Maze Craze Game Board

Making the cards:

On 2½″×3″ construction paper cards write sentences that would use a homonym. Leave a blank where the homonym would go and write the two choices below. For example:

I lost my best _____ of shoes.
     (pear)   (pair)

The _____ is hot today.
     (sun)   (son)

Mother bought me a _____ dress.
     (blue)   (blew)

Playing the game:

The object of the game is to be the first player to reach his home base at the outer corners of the maze. The players place their tokens in the center of the maze. The first player draws a card, reads the sentence on it and fills in the blank, spelling the word to the other players. If he is correct, he rolls the cube and moves his token towards his home base. If he does not choose the correct word on the card he may not roll the cube. When moving through the maze the players may never cross a black line. The first player to maneuver his token to his home base wins.

Lights . . . Cameras . . . Action!

Materials needed:

—20″×30″ poster board
—construction paper
—1 wooden cube with sides 0, 1, 1, 2, 3, skip a turn
—4 tokens, each a different color

Making the game board:

In the center of the board mount a construction paper stage complete with curtains and lights. In each of the four corners of the board place a door with a star on it. These doors designate the actor's "dressing room" or starting place. Make a path of eight stars from each "dressing room" to the center stage. Each set of stars should be a color to correspond with the tokens. Number each set of stars 1 through 8 to show the sequence each actor is to follow. In the open space on three sides of the board attach three 3″×4″ rectangles to show where the playing cards are to be placed. Label one of these "Nouns" and one "Verbs." The third one is not labeled. In the remaining open space write the name of the game. (See Figure 11-14.)
the game. (See Figure 11-14.)

Making the cards:

Divide construction paper into 3″×4″ blocks (approximately 50). In each block write a sentence which contains a word that can be used either as a noun or a verb. Underline that word. For example:

He let the dog out for a *run*.
Run after the ball.
Sue fell on the *step*.
Please *step* into the boat.

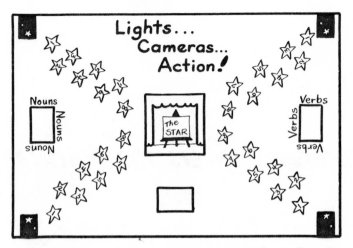

FIGURE 11-14: Lights, Camera, Action! Game Board

Playing the game:

Each player places his token on his dressing room door. The cards are shuffled and placed face down on the rectangle that is not labeled. The first player chooses a card and reads it to the other players. He decides if the underlined word is used as an *action* word, a verb, or as a *naming* word, a noun. He places the card on the proper rectangle. If he is correct he rolls the cube and follows the direction indicated. If he is wrong he does not roll the cube. Play continues around the board until one actor reaches the stage and stardom. He is the winner.

12

Interest Centers the Workshop Way

We have found that the workshop in our classroom provides the children with enrichment of subject areas and the opportunity to explore and experience many different fields. The effort you put forth in creating and accumulating the various materials for the shops is well worth while when you see the children's enthusiastic reactions to them.

To make the development of your shops easier, we have some helpful hints.

1. Plan the activities and games for one shop at a time. You will get bogged down if you try to do too many at one time.
2. Developing your own game is an easy task. All you need is three ingredients:
   a. concept to be learned
   b. theme of the game (baseball, haunted castle, Wild West, outer space, etc.)
   c. catchy title for the game
3. The games aren't limited to one shop. Use the same basic idea for more than one learning concept.
4. To keep the game boards clean, laminate them or cover them with clear Con-Tact paper.
5. To make your game board more attractive and more durable, put colored plastic or vinyl tape on the edges.
6. To make the tokens for the game boards, simply cut dowel rods into 1-inch segments and paint with vivid colors. Shellac all the tokens so the paint won't come off. Put a symbol for the game or initials of the game title on the tokens so they won't get mixed up with tokens from other games.
7. For games requiring dice or cubes to be rolled, purchase a set of

children's wooden blocks from a toy store. Paint and shellac the cubes. Next, write the numbers or words you need on construction paper and glue to each side of the cube. Then shellac the entire cube again.

8. When making playing cards, instead of ruling off every sheet of construction paper you may want to use this quicker method. Using the same size oak tag as the construction paper, rule it off to the size you want your cards. With a sharp cutting knife cut out the inside of each section, leaving a ¼" or ⅛" border on all four sides of each block (Figure 12-1). Place this frame on the construction paper and write the words in the windows. These frames can be labeled as to the size of the cards and used repeatedly.

9. On the back of the playing cards make a symbol or write the initials of the game title so they won't get mixed up with other game cards.

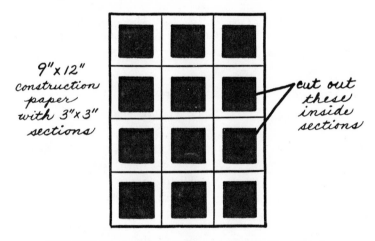

9"x 12" construction paper with 3"x 3" sections

cut out these inside sections

FIGURE 12-1: Window Frame for Playing Cards

10. Laminate the entire sheet of construction paper before you cut the cards apart. Since the construction paper is not ruled off into sections, use a paper cutter to cut the cards.

11. To get away from the "group" connotation, you may want to devise a name to be used in place of "Pat's Group." Some suggestions are:

Pat's Crew	Pat's Club
Pat's Company	Pat's Pack
Pat's Troop	Pat's Family
Pat's Team	Pat's Agency

12. A basic form of bookkeeping can be used for most of the shops. This form consists of a list of all the children's names, and space available

to record the date each one was in the shop and what he did during the allotted time. Another form that can be used is a list of all the activities found in the shop with space available for the child to sign up for an activity. Examples of these forms can be found in Chapter 1.

13.   Keep all the pieces to a game in an envelope, can, box, or jar. The outside of the container can be labeled with the name of the game, a list of game pieces, and directions on how to play.

14.   Activity cards, such as those found in the Creative Writing Shop, Social Studies Shop, etc., can be kept in decorated boxes. It is easier to find a box first and then cut the cards to fit in the box.

15.   To conserve space and assure a neat, uncluttered classroom, the games and activities can be stored in cupboards, boxes, drawers, and on shelves.

This book is a beginning in the organization of interest centers the workshop way. Your workshop should have your personal touch, fitting your and your students' needs. Perhaps some of these ideas for shops may become part of your workshop:

Phonics Shop	Poetry Shop
Ship-Shape Shop	Literature Shop
(exercises)	Craft Shop
Puppet Shop	Ecology Shop
Creative Dramatics Shop	Current Events Shop
Plant Shop	History Shop
Handyman Shop	Who's Who Shop
Music Shop	Travel Bureau Shop

Adding your personal touch to the workshop idea may involve a different type of scheduling system or freedom of movement and choice for your students. Instead of assigning seatwork, try opening the shops so the children can choose and investigate on their own. You may want to set aside a specific time for the operation of the "free" workshop. However you run your workshop, be flexible. Try it different ways. As your workshop develops, you will be able to see the personal growth, self-discipline, and maturity exhibited by your students.

CULMINATING ACTIVITY

A successful culminating activity to the workshop is a year-end carnival or festival for the entire school. This project gives the children the opportunity to display and explain the various activities and units they explored at the shops.

Booths can be made or rented to give this project a really "carnival" atmosphere. Activities and projects completed during the year can be displayed at that shop's booth.

Besides having booths for each shop, there can be game booths interspersed among the display booths.

The children make this project work. They are responsible for making games and prizes for the game booths, creating the shop displays, operating the game booths, and providing explanations for the display booths.

Side attractions at your carnival may be:

—a play production
—a drill team presentation consisting of marching formations and hand movements to music or drums
—a flag corps presentation consisting of movements with flags synchronized to music
—amateur magician
—fortune teller
—artist drawing portraits
—refreshment stand

Set up a schedule for each class to visit your workshop carnival to enjoy the game booths, display booths, and side attractions. It is wise to issue a certain number of tickets for each child to be used for some of the booths and side attractions.

This all-day project is an excellent experience in sharing of knowledge, teaming for a successful common goal, and achieving personal and group satisfaction.

A FINAL WORD

Preparing the activities and games for our Workshop did demand a great deal of time and energy on our part. However, we feel that the children are well worth it. Though we have developed the Workshop in the open-concept classroom, these strategies for learning will work in any traditionally closed classroom! You need not set up the Workshop as such, but simply incorporate these ideas into your daily curriculum as a means of individualizing and enriching the content areas.

It is our strong belief that the interest centers should not be used merely as a free time activity for those students who finish their work early. What happens then to the slower students who especially benefit from this "hands-on" approach to learning? This method of learning offers the students, as well as the teacher, the opportunity for spontaneous interaction and immediate feedback in determining and evaluating the accuracy of their work.

If in some way, great or small, this book has contributed to making your experiences with children more rewarding, we feel we have obtained our goal.

Index